The Rediscovered Writings of Rose Wilder Lane

LITERARY JOURNALIST

The Rediscovered Writings of Rose Wilder Lane

LITERARY JOURNALIST

Edited with an Introduction by

Amy Mattson Lauters

University of Missouri Press Columbia

University of Missouri Press, Columbia, Missouri 65211
Printed and bound in the United States of America

First paperback printing, 2020

ISBN 978-0-8262-2221-3 (paperback : alk. paper)

Library of Congress Cataloging-in-Publication Data

Lane, Rose Wilder, 1886–1968.
The rediscovered writings of Rose Wilder Lane, literary journalist / edited with an introduction by Amy Mattson Lauters.
p. cm.
Summary: "Famous as the editor of her mother's Little House books, Rose Wilder Lane worked for fifty years as a literary journalist, traveling widely and commenting on a broad range of topics. Amy Mattson Lauters has collected examples of Lane's literary nonfiction articles that have been unavailable since their original publication"—Provided by publisher.
Includes bibliographical references.
ISBN 978-0-8262-1721-9 (hard cover : alk. paper)
1. Lane, Rose Wilder, 1886–1968. 2. American prose literature—20th century. 3. Reportage literature, American. I. Lauters, Amy Mattson, 1972– II. Title.
PS3523.A553A6 2007
813'.52—dc22
[B] 2006100672

♾ ™ This paper meets the requirements of the American National Standard for Permanence of Paper for Printed Library Materials, Z39.48, 1984.

Designer: Kristie Lee
Typesetter: BookComp Inc.
Printer and binder: Thomson-Shore, Inc.
Typefaces: Adobe Garamond and Bickham Script

Contents

Acknowledgments

Every project begins with an idea, lurking in the bottom of consciousness over a long period of time until it is encouraged to come to the surface, seek the light, and bloom. In this case, the idea of pursuing study of Rose Wilder Lane began years ago, when a rabid fascination with the "Little House" series of books led to a compulsion to uncover as much as possible about the lives of all those real people on whom the characters were based. When I learned that Rose had been a writer and a journalist, I became curious about the woman who, as far as I knew, was best known as baby Rose in the last book of the series, *The First Four Years.*

Years passed. I became a journalist myself, and then sought a graduate education. It was in a doctoral seminar on women's rhetorical history at the University of Minnesota that I decided to really explore Rose's career and political rhetoric. But it was in a seminar on literary journalism that I finally put the puzzle pieces of her life and work together and concluded that Rose, herself, should be considered a literary journalist. Through this process, of course, guidance and encouragement came from several quarters. Hazel Dicken-Garcia, my adviser at Minnesota, provided her invaluable aid and wealth of resources as I pursued this project while simultaneously studying for prelims and conducting research for my dissertation. Lillian Bridwell-Bowles, the professor who conducted the seminar on women's rhetorical history, encouraged the examination of Rose's life and rhetoric, offering an insight into her character; Nancy Roberts, the professor of literary journalism, not only provided valuable instruction and resources, but also thoughtfully critiqued my position that women in literary journalism, having written mainly for women's magazines that have historically been devalued as media forms, have been largely overlooked in the field.

I have been fortunate in my life to have found wonderful women mentors, and all of them have had a profound influence on me in that they encouraged me to be all I could be and to pursue the stories I thought needed telling. My grandmothers, Elsie Mattson and Fern Bruner; my mother, Linnea Mattson; my aunts, Louise Jensen, Jeanne Anderson, Julie Olsen, and Bonnie Mattson; my sister, Tracy Mattson Wiltrout; and my sister-cousins, Joanne Jensen, Nicole Mattson Kohls, and Sara Mattson, all provided lasting support in my pursuit of telling women's stories. Terri Lescelius, my editor at the *Marinette-Menominee EagleHerald,* gave me the freedom to pursue stories under her watch that started me on the road to graduate school. Karen Riggs, Mia Consalvo, and Tasha Oren, my master's committee at the University of Wisconsin–Milwaukee, not only showed me the ropes of academia, but also opened the door to an academic career I might not have pursued otherwise.

I also want to acknowledge, with thanks, in working on this book, some of my family who aided in the transcription of Rose's pieces from photocopies to electronic forms. Shawn Mattson, Tracy Wiltrout, Jeanne Anderson, and Mike Mattson all helped with the typing. And Suzan Schaefer, at *Woman's Day,* dug otherwise unavailable copies of Lane's articles out of their archives to aid in my research. Thanks also are due to Spencer Howard and the staff at the Hoover Presidential Library. Finally, thanks must be extended to Abigail MacBride and the Little House Heritage Trust for their permission to reprint the articles in this collection.

The Rediscovered Writings of Rose Wilder Lane

LITERARY JOURNALIST

Introduction

In December 1965, the last printed work of Rose Wilder Lane appeared in *Woman's Day,* a women's magazine with which Lane had maintained a long relationship. Called "August in Viet Nam," the lengthy piece described the sights, sounds, and atmosphere of the country into which the United States had been sending soldiers. Lane, at seventy-eight, had been sent by the magazine to Vietnam to explore conditions there. In 1968, just as she was about to resume her journalistic career for *Woman's Day* with a trip around the world at age eighty-one, Lane passed away.

She left behind reams of work that document the career of a literary journalist, one who wrote both fiction and nonfiction printed prose with literary style and technique. She also left her mark on children's literature as the editor of the "Little House" series of books by Laura Ingalls Wilder, Lane's mother. Scholarship about Lane has focused largely on her connection to Wilder, on her relationship with her mother and to the "Little House" books, and, more recently, on her politics as evidenced through her fiction and political writings.[1] A single scholarly biography, released to a storm of controversy, sought to unmask Lane as the true author of the

1. See Ann Romines, *Constructing the Little House: Gender, Culture, and Laura Ingalls Wilder;* John E. Miller, *Becoming Laura Ingalls Wilder: The Woman behind the Legend.* See also Donna Campbell, "'Written with a Hard and Ruthless Purpose': Rose Wilder Lane, Edna Ferber, and Middlebrow Regional Fiction," in Lisa Botshon and Meredith Goldsmith, eds., *Middlebrow Moderns: Popular American Women Writers of the 1920s;* and Julia C. Ehrhardt, "'Stand Entirely on My Own Feet,'" in *Writers of Conviction: The Personal Politics of Zona Gale, Dorothy Canfield Fisher, Rose Wilder Lane, and Josephine Herbst.*

Wilder books and painted a portrait of a woman torn between her own needs and those of her family.[2]

All of these works, however, fail to place Lane and her career in a single, cohesive category. She is a fiction writer; she is a master of children's literature; she is a political rhetorician; she is a journalist. What none of these scholars have done is examine the whole of her work from all its angles, valuing her journalism as much as her literature. This work brings together a collection of Lane's journalism and argues that, taken together, Lane's life and work best fit in the context of literary journalism.

Literary Journalism

Literary journalism draws on a scholarly tradition that lays out writing genres on a sort of spectrum, often with fiction at one end and fact-based news reporting on the other end.[3] But scholars also have begun to isolate writers that do not appear to have confined themselves to one end of the spectrum or the other; their work often falls somewhere in between. Such authors include Stephen Crane, Ernest Hemingway, Theodore Dreiser, Hunter S. Thompson, Dorothy Day, Zona Gale, and Willa Cather.[4] What many of these writers have in common is the use of a start in newspaper journalism to spring into fiction writing of literary quality, particularly with the understanding that such a leap was necessary to being accepted as literati.[5]

But these writers, among others, persisted in creating work that was neither fact nor fiction, in some ways amalgamating the two genres to pro-

2. William Holtz, *The Ghost in the Little House: A Life of Rose Wilder Lane.*

3. See Shelley Fisher Fishkin, *From Fact to Fiction: Journalism and Imaginative Writing in America* (Baltimore: John Hopkins University Press, 1985). Fishkin particularly argues that imaginative writing and journalism should be characterized as distinct, and the boundaries of each redrawn (10, 207–10).

4. A variety of anthologies of literary journalism have been published that include many other writers in this tradition. See, for example, Kevin Kerrane and Ben Yagoda, eds., *The Art of Fact: A Historical Anthology of Literary Journalism* (New York: Touchstone, 1998); Norman Sims and Mark Kramer, eds., *Literary Journalism: A New Collection of the Best American Nonfiction* (New York: Ballantine Books, 1995); and Norman Sims, ed., *Literary Journalism in the Twentieth Century* (New York: Oxford University Press, 1990).

5. Fishkin demonstrates this through highlighting the careers of Walt Whitman, Mark Twain, Theodore Dreiser, Ernest Hemingway, and John Dos Passos, all of whom began literary life as journalists.

duce nonfiction, printed prose of literary quality. Examples include Hemingway's reprints of his many journalistic pieces in his fiction works and Dreiser's lightly fictionalized account of a real-life murder trial surrounding the phenomenon of young lovers and murder in the late nineteenth century in *An American Tragedy.* Gale and Cather appear to have drawn from their journalistic careers for much of their fiction, or used them as a kind of training ground for their careers as fiction writers.[6]

As defined by Thomas B. Connery, literary journalism is "nonfiction printed prose whose verifiable content is shaped and transformed into a story or sketch by use of narrative and rhetorical techniques generally associated with fiction." Through these stories and sketches, authors "make a statement, or provide an interpretation, about the people and culture depicted." Norman Sims adds to this definition by suggesting the genre itself allows readers to "behold others' lives, often set within far clearer contexts than we can bring to our own." He goes on to suggest, "There is something intrinsically political—and strongly democratic—about literary journalism—something pluralistic, pro-individual, anti-cant, and anti-elite." Further, as John E. Hartsock points out, the bulk of work that has been considered literary journalism is composed "largely by professional journalists or those writers whose industrial means of production is to be found in the newspaper and magazine press, thus making them at least for the interim de facto journalists." Common to many definitions of literary journalism is that the work itself should contain some kind of higher truth; the stories themselves may be said to be emblematic of a larger truth.[7]

In order to establish work as literary journalism, therefore, its writer may have at one point worked as a professional journalist. The work must be factually verifiable but must use narrative and literary techniques. Finally, the work must also shed light on the lives of the ordinary people he

6. See Fishkin, *Fact to Fiction,* 140–44, 120–21. See also Elizabeth Burt, "Rediscovering Zona Gale, Journalist," *American Journalism* 12, no. 4 (fall 1995): 444–61; and Carolyn Kitch, "The Work That Came before the Art: Willa Cather as Journalist, 1893–1912," *American Journalism* 14, nos. 3–4 (summer–fall 1997): 425–40, respectively.

7. Thomas B. Connery, preface to *A Sourcebook of American Literary Journalism: Representative Writers in an Emerging Genre* (New York: Greenwood Press, 1992), xiv; Sims, "Breakable Rules for Literary Journalists," in *Literary Journalism in the Twentieth Century,* 34; John E. Hartsock, *A History of American Literary Journalism: The Emergence of a Modern Narrative Form* (Amherst: University of Massachusetts Press, 2000), 13.

or she writes about, in a way that at its heart might seem intrinsically political in its pursuit of a higher literary truth. The work and career of Rose Wilder Lane satisfies all of these conditions.

Finding Rose Wilder Lane

Lane is one of five women in her family who were immortalized as children through works of fiction. A series of books, patterned after the "Little House" series and attributed to her heir, Roger Lea MacBride, documents her childhood and life up until she met her husband, Claire Gillette Lane. Through those books, MacBride often told stories that he had heard from Lane, drawing on the papers she left and on her archive of published material.[8] Sifting the factual Rose Lane from the fictional Rose Wilder is an arduous task, in part because she, herself, was given toward hyperbole when discussing her own life.

What is known, however, is the sketch of her life as she wished it to be known. An autobiography Lane wrote for the Federal Writers Project identifies her as a "plump, Middle-Western, Middle-Class, middle-aged woman with white hair and simple tastes."[9] Born in De Smet, South Dakota, on December 5, 1886, to Laura Ingalls and Almanzo Wilder, Lane grew up in an economically poor household; the Wilders lost their farm in South Dakota after years of successive crop failures. Trial living in Minnesota and Florida also failed. A diary of the journey the family finally took to Mansfield, Missouri, kept by Laura Ingalls Wilder and later published as *On the Way Home,* carries a foreword by Lane, who remembered the trip by wagon vividly. Settled in at what would become Rocky Ridge Farm, Lane appears to have been a precocious child; she read anything she could get her hands on and left school in the middle of terms.[10] At sixteen, she crammed three years of high

8. These titles, all attributed to Roger Lea MacBride, are published by HarperCollins. They include *Little House on Rocky Ridge* (1993), *Little Farm in the Ozarks* (1994), *In the Land of the Big Red Apple* (1995), *On the Other Side of the Hill* (1995), *Little Town in the Ozarks* (1996), *New Dawn on Rocky Ridge* (1997), *On the Banks of the Bayou* (1998), and *Bachelor Girl* (1999). The last four books were released posthumously; MacBride died in 1995.

9. Rose Wilder Lane, "An Autobiographical Sketch of Rose Wilder Lane," Federal Writers Project, 1940, http://lcweb2.loc.gov/wpa/15100107.html.

10. Rose Wilder Lane and Roger Lea MacBride, *Rose Wilder Lane;* William T. Anderson, *Laura's Rose: The Story of Rose Wilder Lane;* Holtz, *Ghost,* 35–38.

schooling into one, to graduate in Crowley, Louisiana, where she had been sent to stay with her aunt, Eliza Jane Wilder Thayer, in order to finish her education. At seventeen, she began work as a telegrapher in Kansas City; shortly thereafter, Lane left for Sacramento, California, to continue that work.

There, she met and married Claire Gillette Lane. It was not a happy marriage, as evidenced through her own autobiographical sketches of that period of her life. The pair traveled extensively, lost a son, and eventually found themselves back in California, where Rose started work with the *San Francisco Bulletin,* working with Bessie Beatty under the auspices of Fremont Older. According to her diaries, Rose started work in 1914 at $12.50 a week; according to her mother's letters (republished in *West from Home*), that salary had tripled by the summer of 1915, when Laura visited the couple in their home on Telegraph Hill.

For Lane, the training at the *Bulletin* was valuable experience. Her diaries show her constant efforts to learn more about the craft of writing; notes about how to write, taken from her reading of various authors, permeate the texts. She also began to develop an ear for dialogue and wit and an eye for active description, which would serve her well in her writing career. Consider this exchange, in the columns of the *Bulletin,* about a kindness contest:

> The worst about this Kindness contest is that it leaves one so defenseless!
>
> "Did you see in the paper—" my friend asks.
>
> "I haven't time to read anything these days but my own copy," I answer, too hastily.
>
> "I pity you, dear," replies my friend—
>
> And I am being kind!
>
> "I love your humor," someone says—
>
> And just as I am beginning the proper deprecating smile—
>
> "It's so entirely unconscious," she adds.
>
> And I—I am being KIND!
>
> "I made this waist myself, every stitch of it," I say with pride.
>
> "Never mind, dear, no one will know it—if you keep your coat buttoned," replies the dear friend who envies me—and when later she asks me how I like her new hat, can I tell her?

No. I am being kind.

I really AM being kind. And still, sometimes I wonder—

Of course, there is five dollars in it for me—if I can be kinder than Josephine Bartlett and several hundred thousand other readers of The Bulletin—

And yet—

Ten whole days of being kind, at any cost—for only five dollars![II]

"What! Me? In a Kindness Contest!" I said, startled. "It wouldn't be fair to the other contestants. I'm always kind."

For I have always gone on the theory that kindness to those you like comes naturally, and unkindness to those you don't like is too much bother. (Pure laziness, some say.) But, then, the other side of virtue is always SOME fault.

"Not being unkind isn't really being kind," Miss Beatty protests.

"But being kind to your enemies is the best way on earth to make them miserable," I reply. "I couldn't be so unkind as to make even an enemy feel those emotions you have when some one angelically forgives you something you don't want to be forgiven. I may enter your kindness contest, but I refuse to be so cruel as to be kind to my enemies."

"It isn't kind to come down to the office with such a gloomy look on your face," Miss Beatty said one morning.

One of the striking things about being in a kindness contest is the frankness of your friends about your every action.

"Take a smile as you'd take medicine. James says no one can be gloomy when the corners of the mouth are turned up," she suggested.

Fascinated by the experiment, I tried it. It works.

Lost in the joys of scientific research, I continued to smile, and slowly felt myself getting happier and happier. I felt kindly toward all the world. I could even have gone through the ordeal of buying shoes without hating the clerk.

All my experiences were like that.

I began by finding that something I was doing was unkind—to my surprise. I learned to undo it—to my profit.

And I have concluded that being kind to others is being kinder to yourself. You get more out of it than the other person does.

II. "The Kindness Contest . . . ," excerpts from the *San Francisco Bulletin,* December–January 1915–1916.

In other words, kindness is the best policy.
Which is a small, contemptible unworthy motive for being kind.
But it's the truth, anyway.
Blame Nature about it, not me.[12]

Another column, written by Lane, hints at her dissatisfaction with her husband:

"Why," said the woman with the interrogative eyebrows [Lane], "Why will men do any of the things they do and then talk about women being the mysterious sex?

"Why will men, who love a smoke more than mother, home, or heaven; who are gloomy, morose, unhappy and ill if they haven't a small bonfire going in the corner of their mouths, why will they NEVER have a match on their persons?

"Why will men whose feet are the largest and unloveliest parts of their anatomy, plainly suited for use and not for ornament, fidget and front and fume until they get those feet on the desk before them, screening the whole of a new fifty-dollar tailored suit?

"Why will man, seized with a sudden panic of neatness on beholding a house, shining with cleanliness, carefully put all the cigar ashes under the pillow when they lie smoking in bed, and conceal the burnt matches inside the pillow cover?

"Why will they furtively slip Nick Carter novels under the bathtub, whence they can be coaxed only with grappling hooks and lyings on one's tummy?

"Why will men go in to a cigar shop to buy cigars and remain there to shake dice for boxes of candy that they do not want and cannot give away, and then smile superiorly at a woman's shopping?

"Why will men marry the women they do and then wish they were the women they aren't?

"Why will men boast that their wives have an equal checking power against the bank account and add triumphantly that the said wives haven't the faintest idea how to draw a check, and then pat themselves on the back for being model husbands?

12. "Always Kind; Out of Race," excerpts from the *San Francisco Bulletin,* December–January 1915–1916.

> "Why will men say proudly that in thirteen years of married life they have had occasion only twice to assert their authority and really improve their wives, and believe it a signal proof of model husbandness, instead of a well-right superhuman self-control on the part of the wives?
>
> "Why will men laugh at women's styles and at the same time wear green hats with crushed silk bands and peacock feathers in back. In short, why ARE men, anyhow?"
>
> Appreciating the value of a climax, or being short of breath, the woman of the interrogative eyebrows stopped.
>
> The woman with the ever-ready answer [Beatty] took up the conversation. "Because," she said.[13]

Her marriage crumbling, Lane continued to write serials, fiction, and nonfiction that ran over successive issues of the *Bulletin,* and she started to make industry contacts with an eye toward a freelance career. She began to ghostwrite autobiographies for such notables as Henry Ford, Art Smith, and then-future president Herbert Hoover, some of which first ran in either the *Bulletin* or in *Sunset,* a California-based literary magazine. As her experience with writing in a variety of genres for a variety of markets grew, her signature style also became more refined, characterized by thick description, active voice, lively dialogue, and absolute adherence to a particular storyteller's point of view. As she pushed forward into the fiction market to earn recognition as a woman of letters, Lane continued to rely on the skills she gleaned as a journalist to tell her stories, and her nonfiction articles remained a small but steady part of her income. As her career evolved, Lane wrote biographies, travelogues, political commentary, news features, short fiction stories, fiction novels, documentary novels, history, and how-to features. The sheer volume and variety of her work makes it difficult to place her into any one category as a writer, but emphasis has been placed in previous scholarship on her fiction writing and on her political commentary.

This book introduces readers to Lane's life through her journalism and argues that her work and career help place her in scholarship not only as an author or political rhetorician, but also as a literary journalist. Literary journalists write both fiction and nonfiction, but key to all their work is an

13. "Why Are Men?" *San Francisco Bulletin,* January 18, 1915.

underlying "truth" that can only be shown through the literary and rhetorical technique used in the writing. Lane infused her writing, both nonfiction and fiction, with her particular ideology of Americanism and individualism, self-reliance, and freedom from government interference, and, in doing so, provided stark commentary on the times in which she lived. While the present volume focuses on her nonfiction printed prose, which best exemplifies her literary journalism and her approach to writing as a craft and career, other scholarship could clearly delineate the infusion of her ideology in her fiction and political commentary.

Each of the stories reprinted here was chosen because it in some way reveals the inner woman behind the text, reveals her particular truths, and encapsulates a watershed moment for her or for the times in which she lived. Together, printed in more or less chronological order, the articles here tell the story of a writer whose first priority, at times, was to put food on her table; a writer whose philosophies stiffened and strengthened into principles that infused all of her work, fiction and nonfiction alike, with American values as she viewed them; and a writer who assumed the mantle of custodian to Americanism through women's arts.

The stories printed here also reveal the development of Lane's signature literary style in her nonfiction work, and each story reveals more about Lane's style and progression as a writer. The selections here also were chosen for their rarity; the reading public has seen none of these pieces since their first printings.

By her own admission, Lane's cultural identity was quintessentially American, middle-class, middle-western, and simple in its tastes. Reading these pieces in succession offers a sense of the woman, her life, and her style. Each stands alone, bearing witness to past eras while espousing timeless values. But read together, they shade in a rainbow of genres that is the signature of a literary journalist.

This work does not provide commentary on Lane's fiction, which has been discussed elsewhere; nor, except where relevant to Lane's career, does it comment on Lane's relationship to Laura Ingalls Wilder. Instead, the goal of this collection is to provide and celebrate the rich evidence for recognizing Rose Wilder Lane's own unique place in history as a literary journalist.

1.

Mrs. Lane Goes to Hollywood

Lane stayed in California through 1918, when her marriage dissolved and her editor, Fremont Older, was forced out of The Bulletin. *"The Bulletin is dead," she wrote in her diary July 20, 1918. "Funeral early in 1919. No flowers. Only members of the family will be present at the interment."*[1] *Her diaries reveal a woman who was clearly depressed over the seeming instability of her life and income.*

But they also show a renewed commitment toward making a career out of writing, and they reflect a self-education course designed to help her succeed not just as a journalist, but as a woman of letters. She lists numerous books on writing in her diaries, reflecting on what she was learning about the craft. "The writer works in the most uncertain, unclutchable material," Lane reflected on July 29, 1918. "Stevenson assumes that a word is a combination of letters, whereas, for the writers' purposes, a word is the meaning attached to it, and this meaning varies in the most delicate, most profoundly important particulars, with each person who hears or reads it writing in collaboration, a passing of meaning from writer to reader. But the value of a word differs, not only from writer to reader, but between the

1. Personal diary, July 20, 1918, Rose Wilder Lane Papers, Hoover Presidential Library, box 19 (hereinafter cited as RWLP).

writer and each of his readers. The writer does not construct a mosaic of definite particles; he tries to paint in clear lines with a rainbow."[2]

The stories in this section, reprinted from* Sunset *magazine, show how Lane was developing her talent at dialogue and thick description.

Twinkle, Twinkle, Little Stars!

(*Sunset* 40, no. 1, January 1918)

This piece is a straightforward news feature about child actors and actresses in the fledgling California movie industry. Already evident are Lane's specific values of simple living and hard work, and her interest in demonstrating the richness of such living. This story also sheds light on early conditions for child actors.

Hot southern California sunshine poured down on the Persian bazaar. It gleamed on enameled nargileh bowls, sparkled among the jewels of dancing girls, deepened the crimson and blue and orange robes of a hundred turbaned Orientals who jostled each other in the open-air café.

Ragged goat-herds and donkey drivers lounged in archways, where their patient beasts stood dozing. Barefooted sweetmeat sellers wandered through the crowd with trays of Turkish pastries and cigarettes. Thin wisps of incense smoke curled up from copper bowls set on the low stage, where a half-naked girl swayed and postured to the strains of throbbing music.

From a balcony hung with Persian rugs C. M. Franklin, directing the latest Fox picture, "Ali Baba and the Forty Thieves," shouted orders through his megaphone, and out of range of the camera his new leading lady, dressed in jeweled breast-piece and chiffon trousers, sat playing with her bare toes.

The leading man approached, munching an apple. He tossed the dangling end of his turban over his shoulder, planted his Turkish-trousered legs wide apart, and looked down at the star. "Gerty," he said paternally, with the superiority of his seven years, "you hadn't ought to do that, you know, now you're a leading lady."

Gerty rolled over on the brocaded cushion. Her eyes widened. "Aw, gimme a bite, Georgie," she said.

2. Diary, July 29, 1918, RWLP, box 19.

"You got your make-up on," he warned, extending the apple. She curled back her painted lips and bit carefully. "Mama didn't say I couldn't eat an apple," she mumbled, with full mouth. "She said I couldn't eat ice-cream."

They chewed for a moment in companionable silence. "After I get through work, then I can eat ice-cream," said the star. "Then I don't care if I spoil my make-up."

"After *I* get through work, then I'm going down to get my new dog," said Georgie. "He's an Airedale dog. Because mama gets my money today, and the man said he would sell him for fifty dollars, and mama says I can keep him in the back yard with the cat."

The stream of dimes which pours into box offices is coined from fundamental human emotions. Love of children is the deepest of these, as the Fox studios have profitably discovered. Since first a loving wife was wronged on the screen, or a drunken husband staggered home to a terrified family, children have played small parts, but it remained for the Franklin boys, as the brothers C. M. and S. A. Franklin prefer to be called, to "star" babies of four and five years.

It paid. It paid so well, indeed, that now the life of the Fox studios in Hollywood revolves around the children. For them great glass-enclosed stages have been erected, rows of miniature dressing rooms built, a schoolhouse and rest-rooms provided, wardrobe rooms filled with tiny garments and feathered head-dresses.

Actors and actresses, directors, cameramen, think habitually now in that mental attitude peculiar to mothers—that attitude of stooping slightly, always to hear the voices of children. But the studio children say little. Small mandarins in stiff brocades, with painted eyelids and painted lips; tiny Persians swathed in heavy turbans and sashes; baby dancing girls covered with grease-paint, in transparent scarfs and clinking bracelets, they move about silently, busy as children always are with their own secret thoughts.

To these babies, dressed in barbaric silks and spangles, fairy tales have become "work." The make-believe world of a child's imagination has been made plaster and wood to them. They do not thrill to stories of magic lamps and obedient genies. They have seen French villages rise where overnight mountain logging camps stood among redwoods. They speak technically of "disappearing scenes." They know that the back of Aladdin's magic palace is rough wooden props and scaffolding for the cameras, that one recalcitrant donkey with two kicks can demolish the Princess' marble halls.

All the values of a normal child's life have become transposed for them. Tragedy which brings tears to the eyes is to lose a make-up box, to blur the crisp lines of red on their lips—horror of horrors!—to spoil a scene. Joy which sets their feet scampering is the voice of the director's megaphone, telling them to go to school.

But the spirit of childhood is as irrepressible as new leaves in the springtime. Work in the studios can not kill it. Work in the studios is carefully guarded against killing it. Indeed, the qualities which make a charming child anywhere are the qualities which motion-picture companies have heaped their piled-up millions by applying modern commercial methods to the old principle that human nature is the same everywhere. And only one person in the world looks with delight on a spoiled child, that person being a child's mother. Therefore, above all things, a studio child must not become an "up-stage."

Had Robert Louis the Beloved been a studio child, he must have written it:

Children you are very clever,
But you must not know it, ever.
You must stay, through all bewild'ring,
Innocent and simple children.

Do not think of insurrection,
Mind the megaphone's direction;
Artless smiles and childish graces
Raise you soon to starry places.

The advice is complicated. But this is an age of complexities, the most bewildering of which must be faced by studio children. In spite of them, they do remain innocent and artless. Georgie and Gerty, bending together over a box of rented kittens in Ali Baba's plaster cave, or sitting on the knee of a ferociously painted "extra man," are still as simple children as though they were not screen stars.

At home they might much more easily become spoiled. The studio children have charm, beauty, and quick intelligences which would make them marked among ordinary children. No fond parents could resist the temptation to "show them off." But at the studios they are surrounded by equally clever playmates, and they work for directors who are chary of praise.

"Gerty! Where's Gerty?" the megaphone calls. Four-year-old Gerty starts from the stall where she and Georgie have been stroking a donkey. Her mother straightens her jeweled head-band, and tightens the coiling gold snakes on her bare arms.

"You remember the steps, Gerty? He wants you to dance, now. Don't forget—your hands on your hips, and turn, slowly—so—You remember what mama told you?" she says anxiously. Gerty bobs her head. The director is waiting. She scampers through the stalls to her place in the wings of the café stage.

A hundred squatting Orientals begin to chatter. The sweetmeat sellers move though the crowd, calling their wares. Out of range of the camera the piano and the violins begin their throbbing music, while the turbaned blacks on the stage beat their cymbals. Over the uproar, across seventy feet of space, the director's megaphone speaks hollowly.

"Gerty, when I blow this whistle you come on, slowly. Look back at the wings. You don't want to dance; they're making you dance. Understand? Then turn and look at Georgie. Georgie, where are you? Get down in front, near the stage. That's it. You keep looking at Gerty. Gerty, you dance and keep looking at Georgie. Dance till I blow the whistle. Then come around front and make your bow, low, clear to the stage. Get up, and put your hands to your head, and sort of stumble. You're tired, you can't dance any more. Then you straighten up again, and smile—smile at Georgie—and go off. Understand?"

A pause. "Gerty, do you understand? I can't hear her. Somebody up there tell me, does she understand?"

Gerty's peacock-feather head-dress, and then her little dimpled face appear from behind a curtain. She nods vigorously.

"All right. Don't make a mistake. We're going to take it. All ready. Camera!"

These are Gerty's stage directions. This is the extent of her rehearsal. Of the meaning of the scene, the thread of the story, she has no more idea than you or I. A Spanish dancing girl, hired for the scene, has given her a few lessons in Oriental dancing. The camera begins to film the picture, the whistle blows. Gerty appears on the stage.

She is afraid. She cowers from the wings, she looks appealingly at Georgie. She begins to dance. Slowly her little arms wave in time to the music, her fingers, drawn to the snake's-head likeness, dart out and draw back. She puts one hand on her head, the other on her small hips, and undulations sweep her body from writhing shoulders to tiny ankles as she circles around the stage and around again.

Stage money flies through the air and falls in showers about her. The crowd is on its feet, shouting, applauding; "Down! Get down, there in the center!" the megaphone bawls. Director Franklin, shaking his fist furiously, calls on the interpreter to manage his men, to make them sit down! They'll spoil the picture! The interpreter, painted and turbaned, dashes into the scene, howling orders.

The whistle blows. Gerty circles to the front of the stage, bows slowly, gracefully, till her forehead touches the boards. She rises, steps back, stumbles, puts her hands to her forehead, almost falls—She casts a piteous smile at Georgie, and staggers into the wings.

"All right, Gerty. You lie down in the shade now till I tell you to get up. Move the camera down front[,] men. We'll take the crowd," says Director Franklin.

That is all. Half an hour later Gerty is sitting on her mother's knee, while her mother inspects her make-up and mends a broken feather in the head-dress. "What do you think of your dance, Gerty?" someone asks.

"I don't know if I did it right or not," she says timidly. "Mama, can I have my ice-cream?"

"Yes, you can have it, after you're through work. You forgot the step I told you, with your hands on your hips, Gerty, but you made up some others that were all right."

Over the heads of the small stars, of course, mother looks at mother with eyes of jealous rivalry. But Mrs. Messinger and her husband do not believe in spoiling children.

A few years ago the Messingers were a comfortable, ordinary family in Spokane. The father was a mill-wright, the mother kept house and cared for the three children. Times were hard in Spokane, and the family moved to Los Angeles. For a time Mr. Messinger found work. He made all the intricate hardwood interior finish for the Pasadena hotel. Then times were slack again, and someone suggested the moving pictures.

"I always had kind of a notion I would like to be in moving pictures," he says, with an embarrassed smile. "I did get a little work, mob scenes and so on. But when I saw that I would never make much of a success at it, I thought, 'Well, the children are bright; maybe they could really do something big in the pictures, and they got a chance to try now, and I'll give them all the help I can.' And now Gerty's a star, and the others are doing well.

"I don't know that we'll keep them in it. When they get into their teens, then they can make up their minds. But anyway, we've given them a good start. And they're all doing well in school, and none of 'em'll get up-stage as long as my wife and I have anything to say about it. We're not folks that have got anything great to feel set up over. Our families have always been good, respectable folks, in comfortable circumstances, but we haven't got anything to make us feel better than other folks, and neither have the children."

Between scenes the children run to school, still in their costumes and makeup. Montessori should approve of that school. It has a comfortable little house of its own, in one corner of the Fox lot, with low green blackboards and small single seats, but it does not stay there. It follows the children wherever they go on location, Mikado and mandarin, Ali Baba and the Princess and the Forty ferocious Thieves, learn geography and wrinkle their painted foreheads over 'rithmetic under trees or beside brooks or wherever else they may happen to be.

So few of the children are of the same age that the three teachers must give each individual training, and while the grades are kept uniform with those of California's other schools, a child may learn as fast as he likes. School to them is fun, a joyous interlude in their bizarre days, and they learn quickly. Ali Baba, for example, who is Georgie Stone when at home with his dog, is already, at seven, in the third grade, and long division worries him not a bit.

Fantastically attired and painted, he runs about all day between the sets and the schoolroom, eating apples from the "property" fruit baskets, knowing each donkey on the lot by name, and enthusiastic about the wild life he leads on the screen.

"Aw, this isn't work!" he says, with a scornful twist of his reddened lips. "It's fun!"

"What are you going to be when you grow up, Georgie?" That insistent, sinister question which nags at the mind which contemplates these children!

"Me?" He considers. "I'm going to be a wild-animal trainer, that's what I'll be! I'll have a big gun, and make it go 'Bang!' Then you'll see the lions stand around, you bet!"

He and Francis Carpenter, aged six, sit on the edge of a property fountain and discuss the relative merits of popguns, quite oblivious of their fantastic surroundings.

But Virginia Lee Corbin, the five-year-old heroine of "Jack and the Beanstalk," gazes both backward and forward upon a stage career. She looks like a Christmas doll, like a picture on a calendar. Indeed, in idle times between engagements, before she entered the moving pictures, she posed for calendars and Christmas cards.

Her mother speaks for her. Virginia herself has an air of having retreated mentally to some quiet place within herself where she contemplates—who knows what pictures of herself or of the world around her?

Her mother was an actress. Before Virginia was three years old she was playing on the big time in "Human Hearts," a popular melodrama. She memorized a part of eighteen pages, and faithfully performed it every night.

"She used to get so tired between acts that I'd make a bed of coats on a trunk and let her sleep," her mother says. "She was always remarkably bright. She is naturally a great dramatic actress. Every part she played was highly emotional—she cried real tears in every scene."

"Human Hearts" played for three seasons. Then Mrs. Corbin found herself at a hotel in Long Beach, where the child attracted the attention of Ellen Beach Yaw.

"Virginia wasn't doing anything at all then but posing for artists and entertaining at hotels. Everyone told me to put her into moving pictures. So I took her to Pathe Freres, and they put her to work right away."

From the Pathe Western she went to Mack Sennett, and now at five she is a Fox star, adding new laurels to those she gained in "Jack and the Beanstalk," by playing the lead in "The Mikado." Reports as to the astounding salary paid her vary greatly, but she has recently ordered for herself a new limousine, to be painted a light blue and upholstered in rose-color, pink being the color she considers most becoming to her complexion.

After all, studio children are what their mothers make them, as all children are. Life in the studios does not greatly change them. In many ways it is a most wholesome environment. All its lasting rewards depend upon intelligence, obedience and health. Hundreds of thousands of dollars are spent upon productions whose success depends upon the physical welfare, the happy minds, and the personal charm of these children, and everything that money or care can provide toward those ends is given them.

The rest must lie with the mothers. When one remembers the character and charm of women like Maude Adams and Mary Pickford, whose childhood was spent on the stage in a far less healthy environment, the supposed demoralizing influences of the studios themselves may be doubted.

Mars in the Movies: The War God Is Filmed and Found Wanting. There Is More Drama Somewhere in Hollywood Than in the Trenches in France

(*Sunset,* February 1918, 39+)

In "Mars in the Movies," Lane interviews legendary film director D. W. Griffith about his attempt to create a battlefield movie. Scholarship on Griffith is limited primarily to discussions about his most famous work, Birth of a Nation, *which he filmed and released in 1915. At this point in his career, Griffith was attempting to create a motion picture from actual battle footage taken overseas during what then was known as the Great War. Today, we know it as World War I. This piece, again written as a straightforward feature, provided Lane with the opportunity to comment, with some subtlety, on the ridiculous expectations that real-life battle should play out well on the big screen. To her, the idea signified a disconnection from the events of the war with its real-life costs. The piece is stark and is rich in detail, as Lane reaches for a voice to express her opinion of the story.*

Children in school are told that no two persons see the same rainbow. It is one of the astounding facts which stun the mind of a child, but as he grows older he learns that is true not only of rainbows but of everything else under the sun and the stars. The chaos of living shifts about upon the fact that the thing seen is in the eye of the beholder.

The Great War is no exception. Twenty billion persons gaze at the life of a planet in a death grapple upon the ruins of a civilization twenty centuries old. It is a world gone mad, some of us wail. It is an heroic effort to save democratic ideals from extinction under a barbarous autocracy, others proclaim. It is a purely economic struggle between two predatory capitalistic classes, cry the socialists. It is an encounter between two opposing ideas of civilization, the professor points out. It is a job we must finish, the soldier thinks grimly, while detonations of great guns and heavens filled with screaming shells speak for him.

Amid this clamor of a new and gigantic Tower of Babel the voice of the moving picture director speaks in its accustomed accents. To David Wark Griffith, producer of mammoth moving-picture spectacles, the Great War appeared the most stupendous setting for a moving-picture which the world has known. Billions of dollars have been spent upon it. A whole continent is the scene. The armies of five great nations are out "on location," moving from horizon to horizon in gigantic panorama.

To film "Intolerance," Griffith rebuilt and wrecked the walls and towers of Babylon. Here at his hand was a world built through twenty centuries of work and hope and dream, wrecking itself. It appeared the greatest opportunity in history for a corps of camera-men.

Probably David Wark Griffith is the only man in the moving-picture world with the vision, the daring and the ability to accomplish the feat he proposed. Innumerable obstacles confronted him. He overcame them all. He won first the consent, then the approval and enthusiastic support of the English and French governments. He and his company, with Lillian Gish, leading woman, Dorothy Gish, ingénue, and twenty camera-men, were the guests of the allied governments at the front, beyond even the farthest outposts of the Red Cross.

His cameras went into the sky, above clouds of shrapnel smoke, with battling aviators. They penetrated the deepest caverns of captured Hindenburg trenches, forty feet underground. They stood in front-line trenches watching with their round mechanical eyes English soldiers going "over the top" to death. Camera-men crawled across No Man's Land under cover of darkness and set them in shell-holes near German trenches, where they were left all day to take the battle-scenes, electric attachments reeling the film past the clicking shutters.

Griffith brought back hundreds of thousands of feet of film, the fruit of a year's work on the big location. They were developed and run off in the projecting room. The camera's verdict was unmistakable. As a moving-picture spectacle the Great War is not a success.

The fault is in poor directing and poor acting. The light effects are not properly worked out. The wars which moving-picture people manage in their Hollywood studios and in the public parks are much better staged.

Take the front-line trenches, for example. They are merely ditches, eight feet deep, cutting through a desolate, shell-torn country. Overhead, high in the air, a few aeroplanes circle like great buzzards. Puffs of white smoke follow them. As far as the camera lens can picture the country it lies bare, in ridges and hollows of raw earth. Nothing moves upon it. The dead men are only heaps of discolored rags.

The trench is knee-deep in churned filth and mud. A sickening faint hyacinth-odor of poison gas mingles with more sickening stenches. There are only a few men in the front-line ranks. They stand isolated, several hundred feet apart, in the mud. They do nothing. They simply stand.

This is no thrilling scene for a moving picture. It is absolutely no good. The men are not actors. They do not register despair, or fear, or hope. They are simply men in soldier's khaki, who stand, waiting.

Even when one is killed he simply crumples up, limply. He does not do a good fall. He does not die dramatically.

On the front, Dorothy Gish, eighteen-year-old ingénue with Griffith's company, saw for the first time a man killed. She was surprised. She had thought it would be a terrible experience which would leave its mark upon her dreams. But she had seen more harrowing deaths played before the cameras in the studios. Unconsciously she was insulated by the moving-picture point of view.

"It wasn't horrible at all," she says, wide-eyed. "I saw him there talking, and suddenly he just crumpled up and slumped down on the ground. He went down just as a suit of clothes would go if no one was left inside them.

"Nobody would do a death that way for the pictures. People would say he was a bum actor."

It was while making his wave along the front in search of better locations that Mr. Griffith penetrated the underground caves dug by the Germans and later captured by the English. With the officer who accompanied him, he went down a shaft to the forty-foot level.

Finally they limped about and walked on solid earth, following the line of the trench across the plain empty of every living thing, stripped of every green leaf. Presently a shell dropped down upon them from the empty sky.

There was only time to hear its shrill thin screech before it struck. It threw up a geyser of mud from the trench. It was a "dud" and did not explode. It was followed instantly by another, which tore a hole in the earth at some little distance.

"By Jove, I do believe they're 'strafing' us!" said the English officer.

Griffith's next recollection is of being in the trench, beneath a covering of earth and branches which had been built as a blind. It was only a foot thick, and no protection, but it seemed a refuge. Shells were still dropping at varying distances around him. There was no one in sight in the trench. The officer had disappeared. Suddenly a voice sounded hollowly at his ear.

"Who are you? What are you doing there?" it said. Behind him, Griffith perceived a wall of masonry, in which was a hole of a few inches in diameter. He peered through it, and saw at its other end the face of a strange officer, separated from him by six feet of cement wall.

"I'm a moving-picture director, looking for locations," he replied.

"It is my duty to arrest you," said the officer.

"Come and do it," Griffith answered eagerly, longing for the shelter of the solid six foot wall. But the only exit from the cement wall in which the officer was stationed was several hundred feet away in No Man's Land, on which the shells continued to fall with increasing fury.

The pit had originally been built by the Germans as a base for a big gun. When the trenches were captured by the English it became an observation station. Its entrance still lay between the lines, near the German trenches. The officer entered it by night, and remained there all day with no possibility of escape. At intervals the Germans shelled him.

Around him was a curving wall of gray cement. Above him was a circle of gray sky. Into that circle the German gunners endeavored to drop one of the screeching shells. It was an incessant and monstrous game of tiddle-dewinks, on which his life depended. He sat all day with a telephone receiver and mouthpiece clamped to his head. Now and then he spoke a few numbers into the mouthpiece, and five miles behind him a gunner alerted the angle of his gun by a fraction of an inch and mechanically fired into space.

That was all. If that be drama, no moving-picture audience will pay its dollars to see it on the screen. What would it see? A man with a telephone receiver at his ear.

They do these things better in the moving pictures. There a gallant officer leads his fine young troops to battle with flashing sword and waving arm, and close-up of the fighting light in his eye. There the arms meet on open ground, with crash of cavalry and waving flags. There the massed infantry is cheered to the charge, and "the lean, locked ranks go roaring down to die."

Alas, the moving-pictures were born too late. What a location the Civil War would have been for an energetic and enterprising director!

"You can't get a good picture of men going over the top," says Griffith. "In the first place, they always do it when the light is bad. Usually about four o'clock in the morning.

"The night before an attack the frontline trenches fill up. Men keep coming in from the rear until they are packed as thickly as they can stand. They simply wait, then, until they get orders to advance. It is dark. You can't see them in the darkness, and naturally arc lights are out of the question.

"There's not much talking. They're pretty quiet. Now and then, someone will light a cigarette, but of course they must be careful not to show the light. Along toward morning the barrage fire begins, and then a little later, in that gray uncertain morning light when you see nothing distinctly, the men are ordered out.

"They don't go over the top with a cheer, or in a rush. They simply climb out and walk across toward the German trenches. There's no thrill or excitement in it. The officer goes ahead with an eye on his wrist-watch. He knows the rate at which they should go, behind the barrage fire. If they make time too quickly he stops them for a minute or two, and then they go on. Of course they are under the infantry fire.

"When they get to the enemy trenches they simply drop into them and kill anyone who's left there still fighting. There are very few men in the front-line trenches, and the big guns clean them out pretty thoroughly before an attack. If there is any hard fighting, it comes later at the second-line trenches. But usually the advance stops with the capture of the first line. Then our men dig themselves in, move up their own second line behind them, and wait until time for the next attack."

Griffith got several hundred feet of this modern version of the battle-charge, but his eye lights with no enthusiasm as he speaks of it. The audience will see the result for itself, he says wearily, when the big war picture is on the screen in January. Nor did the difficulties of filming the Great War end with the taking of these pictures of battles badly directed, badly lighted and poorly acted. In the projecting room, new troubles arose.

Under shell fire a camera-man had been filming the action of the great batteries, thirty-five monster guns wheel to wheel, rising, recoiling, rising again, in clouds of powder smoke, with a roar which shook the air and the ground. It was a magnificent spectacle, the iron heart of the huge machinery of a machine-fought war.

While the film was racing past the snapping shutter of the camera, a German shell struck. The earth where it fell rose in volcanic eruption of dust and debris. A moment later the new-made crater appeared where had been two officers of artillery standing on solid ground. The officers had disappeared.

It was magnificent. It was great stuff. The camera-man had not lost his nerve; he had continued grinding steadily. The film had recorded it all. But in the projecting room it was cut.

The picture was spoiled by the arm of one of those officers. It had been flung, a torn-off, bodiless arm, across the scene in front of the camera. It showed plainly. There were other details. The picture was too realistic, too horrible. Even though it passed the board of censors, audiences would never stand for it.

Every point of view has its own advantages. If all the world is but a moving picture show and all the men and women merely character-parts, there is consolation in the fact that the poor moving-pictures are not booked for long runs. Griffith believes, therefore, that this is the last war. For a year he has seen it in all its phases, from the Court of St. James to the mud of the front-line trenches in Flanders, and he asserts that this is the first of all wars which carries in itself the germs of destruction of all warfare. It is too dull to be repeated.

"All the glamour has gone," he says. "All the magnificence of the maneuvering armies has passed. The armies do not maneuver any more. They go to live in a ditch and stick there (literally) until relieved by other troops. The life of a soldier in a modern war is the life of an underpaid, overworked ditch-digger compelled to live in danger and discomfort.

"The infantry seldom see what they are shooting at. The artillerymen never see their targets; they sight the guns by mathematics. The courier on the foaming charger is replaced by the desk telephone. The generals are almost never on horseback. They fight their battles in an office with an oil-cloth map and draughtsmen.

"All in all, the life of the modern soldier is as dull and monotonous and tedious as the life of the dullest civilian."

The picturesqueness is quite, quite gone. In other words, war is no longer a moving-picture with martial music by the orchestra.

How I Became a Great Actress: Ten Minutes in a Bar-Room with "Doug" Fairbanks the Optimist

(*Sunset,* 4 April 1918, 35+)

This feature about Hollywood focuses on Lane's visit with Douglas Fairbanks on the set of one of his many films. Her interview led to an opportunity to be an extra in the film, and her vivid description of the experience is telling. Here, too, readers can see that Lane is finally using her own voice to tell the story. The use of first-person made it easy for her to focus on one point of view in the telling. This use of point of view is something that clearly distinguishes later pieces; using one lens to tell a story offers subtle insights into the total story. It is also a device Lane begins to use for writing nonfiction, showing readers that despite the content, each is definitively told through a gatekeeper. The following story also illustrates Lane's sense of humor and sheds light on an early screen legend and the process of creating silent movies.

It all happened because Douglas Fairbanks is a philosopher.

One would not think it to look at him. But it has long been an axiom in masculine discussions of women that we like best to be praised for those things which we do not appear to be, and the great discovery made by feminists is that everything men have said of us is true—of themselves.

Therefore it was not surprising to see Douglas Fairbanks standing in the wreckage of an old French inn, still panting from slaughtering fifteen men with his sword, his feet, and a poker, eager to talk philosophy.

"'Laugh and Live' is your philosophy?" said I. "Obviously, it isn't 'Laugh and Let Live.'"

He laughed, mopping at the blood which trickled down his cheek, spoiling the grease-paint. Behind him seven men struggled to crawl from beneath a heavy oaken table which he had overturned upon them, and we heard the stern voice of Allan Dwan, director, commanding, "Men that are dead, stay dead! We're not through with the scene."

"Yes, I'm very fond of philosophy," said Douglas Fairbanks. "Spencer, Locke, Schopenhauer—all those fellows. I'm very fond of them all."

"And Kant?" said I.

"Kant? Oh, yes. Yes, Kant, of course. I'm very fond of him, too. And Orison Swett Marden. Orison Swett Marden! He's the chap to read when you're feeling blue!"

I repeated the name, stunned. "He's the man who edited 'Success' until it failed, isn't he?" I said feebly.

"Yes. Now he's a real philosopher!" said Douglas Fairbanks. "He's got the right idea. Anybody can succeed in anything he undertakes, if he goes after it hard enough. Just be cheerful. Just laugh, and get up and go at it again every time you're knocked down, and you can do anything."

"Anything?"

"Anything," said the optimistic philosopher, firmly. "Ask for what you want, that's the secret of it. Ask for it, don't wait for it to be handed to you. Be determined. And cheerful. And you'll get anything in the world you want."

"Then," said I, "I'll supe in this picture."

It was certainly a moderate demand. A small thing to ask, from all the riches in the whole round world. A small thing to ask, even from the riches of Douglas Fairbanks. I had not even demanded the leading part in the film. My wish, perhaps, was too moderate. Certainly, for the moment, the author of "Laugh and Live" seemed surprisingly taken aback.

Allan Dwan, lounging against a table beside us, laughed aloud. His laugh was distinctly registered on the stunned air before the famous Douglas Fairbanks smile returned. "We'll put you on!" said Allan Dwan.

"We certainly will!" said Douglas Fairbanks. And, with what seemed to be a happy inspiration, he added, "We'll put you on in the bar-room scene. Of course, it'll be pretty rough—one of those knock-down-and-drag-out fights. You know. You've seen me do 'em. I'll try not to hurt you, but you won't object to getting smashed up a little, will you? I can't always be sure where I'm going to land, you know, when I really get started."

He looked at me with serious concern. Allan Dwan also gazed seriously upon me through his round tortoise-shell-rimmed glasses. "The company will pay your doctor bills," he said encouragingly. "We do that for all our extra people. If you get any teeth knocked out, or anything like that, I promise it won't cost you a cent."

"I wouldn't mean to hit you," Douglas Fairbanks further explained. "It's only when bottles and chairs and tables get to flying around—"

There was an anxious pause. But it was not I who felt the anxiety. "I don't mind," I said blithely. "When do you take the scene?"

The two men looked at each other. But Douglas Fairbanks' philosophy should delight William James. It works.

"Well, I suppose I'd better take her over to the dressing-rooms and have her made up," said its out-bluffed author, in a tone of mingled humor and resignation. "I suppose you had," said Dwan.

Douglas Fairbanks' dressing-room suite is part of the long, low, frame building which runs down one side of the Lasky "backlot." We passed through a cobbled street in a Bulgarian town, stopped to wave to Wallace Reid, who was entering a saloon in the wilderness of Music Mountain, cut diagonally through the dismantled New England village in which Mary Pickford played "Rebecca of Sunnybrook Farm," and came through a narrow little street of Japanese paper houses to the dressing-rooms shaded by a row of California pepper trees dripping with crimson berries.

Douglas Fairbanks' door opens on a bare, business-like room, furnished with a long mirror, a shelf covered with neat make-up materials, a desk stacked with papers, and a silent, efficient Japanese valet. No time is lost in that dressing room, no time is spent in the idle gazing at wall decorations.

Fairbanks' favorite pictures are Remington's, but the only quality of them which he brings to the studios with him is their energy. "Anything that is worth doing is worth doing quickly," is apparently his creed.

Things move when he is there. They move rapidly. He goes through the life of the Lasky studios like one of the summer dust-whirls which rise on the broad plains of the Middle West, gay, whimsical, easy-going things to see, but instantly starting something wherever they touch.

Before the Japanese valet had produced an extra make-up box, which he did as by legerdemain, "Doug" Fairbanks' wig was off, his face covered with cold cream, an assistant director had appeared in answer to his call, introductions, explanations had been made, and the Fairbanks smile disappeared behind vigorous scrubs of a towel as I departed for an extra dressing-room.

"Be ready in fifteen minutes," he called, as the screen door closed behind us. And in fifteen minutes we found him, in fresh make-up and costume, in the midst of the bar-room scene.

He had an audience. As crowds are attracted to a street fight, so the people of the Lasky studios gather about Doug Fairbanks' set. Other companies are lounging about in the wilderness of sets beneath the high glass roofs of the Lasky stages, waiting for the star, for the director, for the carpenters, for a change to be made in a tropical garden or for the wagon-load of salt to arrive for an Alaskan scene. There is no waiting in the Fairbanks company. Something is happening there, happening briskly every moment.

No one asks, "Is Doug working today?" They listen. Across the usual clatter of carpenters' hammers and moving furniture there sounds a crash, a bang, the smash of breaking wood and falling walls, the yells of a mob in combat. Yes, Doug is working. From all sides people hasten to watch the devastation.

There was no time now for conversation. Doug was working. He stood in a group of twelve men, roughly dressed "extras" gathered between four dingy board walls to learn how they should die. He struck at this one and that reflectively, he measured the walls and the distances from partition to partition with a considering eye. He consulted with Spike Robson, ex-lightweight champion of England, now his boxing partner and extra man.

Allan Dwan, solemn-eyed behind his large round spectacles, sat in a chair beside the cameras, watching and making suggestions which were instantly captured in shorthand by his stenographer.

"Here, that's too many men left alive. I only want four. Kill off another one. You in the red shirt, get under the table when the row starts, and stay there. You're drunk, and I don't want you to forget it.

"Look out for the chair, Spike. I want a dead, hard fall, a little nearer the camera. That's it."

This was rehearsal. It continued perhaps ten minutes.

"All right, Doug? All right. Get into your places. Off stage, Doug, if you're ready. Camera!"

The steady click-clicking began. Then into that peaceful bar-room scene, where men lounged talking against the bar, and others poured strong brown tea from bottles at the little tables, came charging the hero of the play.

He seized Spike Robson, that stalwart ex-champion of the ring, by his sturdy shoulder, and jerked him to his feet. Spike struck out wildly. "Punch!" commanded Fairbanks, doing it. "Get some pep into it. Hit me! Hit me, if you can!"

Slam! Smash! Smash! Thud! "They're not really *doing* it?" I gasped, but no one heard me. The crowd behind the camera was on tip-toe; in the set the extras were getting to their feet overturning chairs as they came. "Ugh!" Fairbanks grunted, behind a blow. And Spike Robson, fairly struck on the jaw, rocked on his feet and came down with one heavy smash, like a falling tree.

It was a fall to make a camera-man grin with joy. We behind the cameras whole-heartedly admired Spike Robson's work.

But Doug was still fighting. Forgotten underfoot lay the redoubtable Spike, while destruction raged above his head. One man went down—two, three. A chair, hurtling above the bobbing heads, crashed against the wall. Doug was on a table, throwing bottles. He was hanging from the gas-fixture, kicking right and left. He was on top of a partition, stabbing downward with a chair-leg. He leaped six feet to a window-ledge, and stopped to laugh. He dropped into a passage-way, and down came the walls upon the furious crowd.

"Cut!" said Allan Dwan. The camera stopped. Calm fell upon the wreckage of what once had been a bar-room. The chairs were torn apart, the walls were down, the bar was a mass of splintered wood, and fragments of broken wax bottles littered it all. Feebly, beneath shattered boards and toppled tables, the extras came crawling out.

"Here, quit bleeding all over the place! We want to use this scene again," the assistant director remonstrated. "Get off the set if you've got to bleed!"

One of the extra men stood gazing with an expression of bewildered surprise at three of his own teeth. He held them in one palm, and with a finger of the other hand he incredulously explored the gaping place in the upper jaw where they had been.

I saw this in one swift glance, and I did not look again until he had obediently taken his bleeding mouth from the set. "You don't mean—it can't be—were his teeth actually knocked out?" I said, my throat contracting.

"Why, sure!" said someone, in a matter-of-fact tone. And added, in unstinted admiration, "Doug does everything earnestly."

"You can't help things like that in this sort of work," Allan Dwan explained. "Of course Doug doesn't like to have it happen. But we'll pay the dentist's bills."

Then, amid irrepressible mirth, it was discovered that Spike Robson still lay prone and dazed upon the floor. His marvelous fall was not a masterpiece of acting. He had been knocked out.

"Knocked out—knocked out cold on my feet—" he repeated, amazed. "Cold—on my feet! Well, whu' d' you know—Knocked out!"

For some time he went about uncertainly, repeating the words, apparently listening to them to see if they sounded true.

I was hearing them for the third time when Allan Dwan turned suddenly to me. "All right," he said, briskly, "Ready for your scene?"

A brief panic clutched me. I realized, too late, that Doug Fairbanks' philosophy, like its creator, possessed some of the qualities of a buzz-saw. Why had I not remained satisfied with older philosophies less uncertain in their practical conclusions?

"Y-yes," I replied. "What am I to do?"

"Nothing much. It's just a little scene." Allan Dwan's glance gathered in the other extra girl who was to play it with me. "You sit here at this table, that's all. You're tough girls. Doug's going to start a row, and he's always polite to the ladies. He'll come over and tell you about it, before he begins. Then when the fight starts you get out, that's all."

Doug Fairbanks, carefully patting with his handkerchief the tiny beads of sweat which stood out through his grease-paint, added another bit of counsel.

"Don't make a smooth, continuous movement for the pictures. Move by little jerks. Play slowly. Every time you make a movement, pause just a flicker of time to let it register. You won't get it over if you don't."

We sat at the little table. I was given a cigarette, my hat was pulled askew. This I was informed, made me a perfect "tough girl" in appearance. It was said as a compliment.

The Kleigs lights were turned on. They poured upon us a blinding hot glare in which my very eyelashes seemed to sizzle and grow crisp. I blinked.

"Don't close your eyes," said Allan Dwan. "Ready? Camera!"

The clicks of that relentless machine merged into a slow, steady purring. I became as a combination of a mesmerized mouse and a charmed bird, under the double spell of glowing snake's eyes and a cat's throaty song of triumph. Out of the spell came the voice of Allan Dwan, moving me miserably by its commands.

"Talk to each other. Pretend to say something. You're bored. Fine! Yawn again. Go on, Doug."

Douglas Fairbanks appeared at my elbow. He bowed. He smiled the famous Douglas Fairbanks smile.

"So really, ladies, awfully sorry, of course, regrettable necessity, hope will not inconvenience, unfortunate, most unfortunate really and all that sort of thing, do you understand?" said he urbanely.

Allan Dwan's voice went smoothly on. "You don't get him," said he.

"So if unhappily, very sorry I'm sure, hope you will pardon, must be," said Douglas Fairbanks.

"Wha—what?" I said.

"Very well, ladies, so happy acquaintance, trust untroubled, good-by, good-by, good-by," said Douglas Fairbanks, bowing and smiling and bowing again. And he went away.

"Tell each other you don't know what he was driving at," said Allan Dwan.

"What was he driving at?" said I to the other girl.

"Awfully funny guy, what do you know about that?" said she.

"Look here! Look here! Look this way, quick!" cried Allan Dwan. I looked. I remembered that I was to look at a fight, but there was no fight. I reflected that I must look as though I were looking at a fight, and never having watched myself look at a fight, I did not know how to do it.

It was then that Allan Dwan threw the first bottle. It smashed on the wall above my head. I ducked the second one. The third one struck the edge of the table. After that I lost count.

Somewhere, out of the crashing, came one welcome sound. "Get out!" said Allan Dwan. I did so. The last bottle just missed me.

When things settled into place again I found that I was warmly shaking Douglas Fairbanks' hand. He was saying, "Great! Fine! Splendid!" The famous Douglas Fairbanks smile was fully in evidence. "You certainly did register fright!" said he. "I've never seen it better done! Why, when that first bottle just missed you, you became a great actress!"

"It was good. It was very real!" beamed Allan Dwan. The pleasure seemed general among all the crowd behind the cameras. I saw not the slightest trace of the professional jealousy of which we hear so much.

The cameras were being moved to another position. Dwan was placing the extra men for a close-up, dictating in an undertone to his stenographer between commands. The Douglas Fairbanks company was rushing on with its work. I said good-by to the optimistic philosopher, and watched him nimbly scale a wall and sit on the cross-beam, radiating energy and healthy good spirits. Then I fled to the dressing-rooms.

"Good-by! You'll find your money waiting for you in the office!" Dwan called after me.

I did not get it. It will be a pleasure all my life to reflect that the Douglas Fairbanks company owes me five dollars, earnestly earned by supeing with Doug Fairbanks.

But the next time I saw Allan Dwan he assured me that I could play extra parts with the company any time I liked. Which seems to prove that there is something in the Douglas Fairbanks philosophy, unless it proves the injustice of a world which denies to some what it gives to another who does not want the gift.

2.
Mrs. Lane Writes about the War

World War I shook the foundations of national and international expectations, killed off a great many of the world's young men, and left many people disillusioned about their own governments. The world stood on a cusp of enormous changes, and Lane, who lived and worked in Europe between the wars, was at their center. In September 1918, Lane had received a telegram requesting that she work for the Red Cross publicity bureau in London. "Work would be magazine writing," she wrote in her diary.[1] *Although "the Great War" was over before Lane could get overseas to take the job, the assignment yielded some story leads that were sold to* Sunset *and to national women's magazines. Lane had thrown herself into her writing work, and her diaries and correspondence show a woman driven by the need to continually do more to improve her work and to earn cash.*

The Girls They Leave behind Them

(*Sunset,* November 1918)

Lane's job throughout much of her journalistic career was to provide the "woman's perspective" on important national and international events.

1. Diary, RWLP, box 19.

Women's perspectives had gained saliency during the Great War; women's work on the home front during the war was heightened and respected. Women would be granted the vote in 1920. The following piece deals particularly with the problems of girls and women in a society responding to war with rapidly changing norms. What could have been a short feature about the Young Women's Christian Association became, in Lane's hands, a commentary about the social questions facing women of 1918.

> And now I'm bound for Brighton camp,
> Kind Heaven may favor find me,
> And send me safely back again
> To the girl I've left behind me!

It is an old-fashioned song, almost forgotten today, and it was sung by the old-fashioned soldier of half a century ago, who shouldered his musket and marched away to the music of fife and drum, leaving the girl behind him. In those days it was woman's part to be left behind, safe in scented garden or dim parlor. Clarissa, in flowered hoop-skirt and rose-wreathed bonnet, gave a last brave smile to the soldier she might not see again, and turned back to bear her share of war's agonies in bereaved and empty days of waiting.

Life and death, courage and faithfulness and love, remain the same through the centuries, but all outward things change. The khaki-clad youth who entrains for war today carries in his heart the picture of a girl, just as his grandfather did, but he has not left her waiting with clasped hands for his return.

She may reach France before him; she may put on overalls and go into a factory; she may be running an elevator or handling a street car, or managing the business; she may have enlisted as a yeomanette, or she may be driving the tractor-plow. But she has not been left behind. She is in the war, too, and whether for better or worse, he will not find her the same girl when he comes back.

There is no normal girlhood left in the civilized world. Women today are in the swirl of the world-wide whirlpool; they have been swept from safe moorings of home and habit as ruthlessly as their sweethearts and brothers.

At the end of our first year of war a million and a half American women were working on war orders. For every man who has left his job to put on khaki, a woman has left her home to step into the warfare of business or industry. Ten million women are now wage-earners in the United States, and millions more are pouring into vacant places in factories and offices.

Our men are going over-seas, millions upon millions of them, leaving the girls to loneliness and work and new temptations. Some day these men will come back, to find their women changed by many experiences, and somehow, together, the soldier and the working girl must make the America of the future.

There are many organizations that are for the soldier. The Government, the Red Cross, the Y.M.C.A., the Salvation Army—innumerable organizations civil and military—care for his health, his amusements, his education, his ideals. From the beginning of our part in the war the thought and efforts of the nation have been centered upon him.

But the great army of girls and women marched out from the shelter of normal routine into chaos. It was a new phenomenon in warfare, and no provision had been made for it.

Overnight peaceful communities became war-industry centers, crowded with women. Munitions plants and uniform factories arose, filled with women. Around army cantonments, in fields that had been open country and farm land, cities suddenly appeared, and into them poured women.

There were earnest, heart-sick girls, bravely taking up the work their men had dropped; there were mothers and young wives, hastening to the camps for last meetings with their soldiers; there were factories filled with women in towns too small to give them living room; there were thousands of school girls fringing the cantonments, threatening in their blind young enthusiasm the demoralization of the soldiers and the wrecking of their own lives.

Laws and customs change more slowly than life; it is always the task of a government to keep up with the changing lives of its people. War had suddenly disclosed a thousand new angles to the half-disregarded "woman problem," and harassed governmental departments threw up their hands in despair and called for help. Our government, already confronting the colossal task of changing a huge, peaceful, industrial nation into a war-machine, was taken unawares by the emergences of these millions of women from the homes in which they refused to be left behind.

Women were needed to win the war; they could not be sent home. The glib consignment of woman to her old place was quite forgotten in the sharp necessity for her services outside that shelter. But no provision had been made for her outside. The situation was too much for department heads; only women could handle it, and only one organization of women was ready at hand with partial equipment for handling it. The government appealed to the Young Women's Christian Association.

If there was ever a time when the Y.W.C.A. saw religious ideals as separable from social service, that time has gone into the past with other outworn things. In the flux and change of human affairs caused by the world catastrophe, the organization kept and increased its flexibility.

It took up the task of keeping the values of fine girlhood safe from the dangers of war-time. The walls of the home were broken down; the old shelters were gone. America must become one great home, where every inexperienced girl battling with unknown forces should be steadied and helped. The Y.W.C.A. is endeavoring to be a tactful and understanding mother to a million daughters, each with her own traits of headstrong willfulness or clinging helplessness or ignorant self-confidence.

In the cantonment towns even the very youngest girls have quite lost their heads in the war excitement, and more than one mother needs help in handling her own small daughter. When thousands of handsome young khaki-clad heroes suddenly appear in her village, every little girl thrills to the tip of her hair-ribbon bow, and independence riots in her veins.

"What do you like to do after school?" a teacher in San Pedro asked her pupils, shortly after three thousand soldiers were quartered there, and one of the school girls answered unconsciously for thousands of others.

"I do as I please," she replied. "If I didn't, I wouldn't do it."

Every cantonment, as it rose, was fringed with such self-confident, independent misses in their teens, palpitating with excitement, hopeful of winning the admiration of some lonesome soldier-boy. Any girl who couldn't do that was an awful slow-poke!

"Hmp! A girl isn't much good if she can't pick up a different fellow every night since the soldiers came!" said a blithe young San Diego girl, flushed with her own happy triumphs.

The situation was too much for any single mother to meet. However nicely brought up her little girl might be, no one likes to be thought slow and stupid and unattractive. Overnight, in all the cantonment towns in America, all the standards of little-girlhood among its mates has changed.

It is a hardy grown-up who lives counter to the public opinion about him, and what little girl in school could be controlled in acts and ideas by vague talk of good taste? All her future standards of life, the sweetness of her youth, the long years before her, might be at stake, but she could not see it. Her eyes were blinded by flags and music and khaki-clad ranks of soldiers, and her ears were filled with the boasts of other little girls.

The answer of the Y.W.C.A. to the problem is the Community Center, and the Community Center is a club house for the "teen-age" girl. In some cantonment towns these club houses wait like benevolent spiders to snare the little girl, who does not suspect that she is technically called "teen-age." She is lured by dancing classes, by gymnasium work, by attractive rooms where she can meet her chums and plan picnics, or knit for the soldiers, or give parties on Saturday nights.

She does not know that she is given these club rooms to keep her from walking up and down the streets after school and picking up a soldier who will buy her an ice-cream soda; if she knew it she would tip-tilt her independent little nose and leave those rooms empty, and she does not leave them empty. She crowds into them, and there she finds all her young energies absorbed in fun that has nothing to do with too-precocious experiments in love.

The "teen-age" girl's older sister has other problems. She has gone to work. The speeding-up of industry since the beginning of the war has drawn her into the new factories and munitions plants and government offices. The home life of these older girls, in already overcrowded cities, was the last thing considered by the men whose great job was rushing out the materials for making war. The machines must have adequate floor and roof space; munitions, clothing, equipment must be poured out for the first soldiers who hastened over-seas to block the way to Paris. Thought for the girl-workers could come later.

Meantime the girls walked the streets looking for rooms; they took what they could, and came home tired at night to sleep in shabby, high-priced, poorly ventilated places. They were scattered haphazard through the cities, wherever they could find lodging. Their chance for normal, healthy, pleasant girlhood was gone.

If the Y.W.C.A. had had money enough, it might have built model homes for all these new colonies of women workers. At first it could only advise the governmental authorities to build such homes. It supplied housing experts, who made a study of the situation and of women's requirements, drew up a definite plan, and submitted it to the Secretary of War and to the chairman of the housing committee of the Council of National Defense. Then, as a demonstration, the Y.W.C.A. began to build a model home for girls at Charleston, S.C., where the housing situation is especially bad. And in this home it is putting emphasis not only upon pleasant living and sleeping rooms, but also upon recreation.

If girls are to become wholesome women they need fun as keenly as they need rest and food. We have learned that the soldier must have his healthy amusements, and when girls become workers we learn that the workers must have it.

In five other centers the Y.W.C.A. has built or rented houses as emergency shelters for 440 girls. Ten million women are working, but an organization of three thousand persons can not at once re-make an industrial nation covering half a continent. The Y.W.C.A. is doing as much as it can do to help conditions.

It has organized hundreds of room registries, where girls are directed to the best rooms obtainable, in houses investigated by its staff; it has established 127 recreation club centers in industrial districts; it has built sixty-one Hostess Houses in army cantonments, to care for mothers and wives and sweethearts who follow their soldiers to camp.

And all the weight of its great influence is behind its effort to give America's girls new ideals to fit the new conditions.

"The need to work is real—as real for women as for men," the Y.W.C.A. says through its Social Morality propaganda. "Once the home had enough to do to keep its daughters busy all the time. But with fewer things for women to do at home, they have felt the need to go outside and seek paid work. A good job stimulates.

"Go to the great-hearted big sister of all women, Olive Schreiner. Read her book on 'Woman and Labor,' in which she pictures how women have become parasites in the past and how they may regain a self-respecting position in the future. This can only be done through 'labor—and the training that fits us for labor.'

"The census shows us that one-third of the women of working age in the United States are engaged in earning money for self-support. Every ten years a census is taken; and every ten years the census shows a growing number of women added to the 'gainfully employed.' Once it was one-seventh; then, one-fifth; then, one-fourth, and now, one-third. When you are ten years older, what will the proportion be? Maybe, one-half. No wonder we have forgotten to be ashamed of our jobs!

"How long will the girls continue working? 'That,' replies the census, 'is hard to say.' Once we thought it was seven years, but times have changed. Many women of middle age are in industry today. Over four million women in the prime of life are earning their living. And a million and a half who have passed forty-five are still in paying positions—a grandmothers' brigade of workers! Wartime and the years that follow will call on many women of various ages to be self-supporting. Who can say what she may be doing ten or twenty years from now!

"How many girls over fifteen will some day be married? 'We can not foresee the effects of war,' replies the census, 'but in times of peace, about three-fourths should be married some day.' Marriage, then, is another thing which girls must look forward to. No girl can be sure that she will not be one of the married majority and many girls today are not ashamed to say they intend to marry.

"Self-support makes a woman more honest in marriage. If she frankly faces marriage, she must face with equal frankness her own responsibility for making that marriage a happy one.

"Mothers of families who have paid their own way for years are not likely to waste the family income. If marriage may be ranked 'a job' the women capable of self-support need not be ashamed of it."

Every intelligent woman who cares for a girl gives her, with shelter and food and safety, something of her own soul, something of idealism. If the Community Centers, the Recreation Clubs, the Hostess Houses, the room-registration bureaus, the model homes, the Vacation Houses, are the material side of the Y.W.C.A. work, the Big Idea behind it all is its soul.

And it is through the Y.W.C.A. that the women of America are working to help the girls of America, thrown by the war into new ways of living.

It is indeed a long time since the men of our nation marched away to war, singing, "The Girl I Left Behind Me." They are going away to war again, in numbers undreamed of and countless, and though each of them leaves his heart behind him with his girl, he leaves his job with her, too. His song is, "I don't know where I'm going, but I'm on my way." Or sometimes, with something of pathos to an imaginative ear, he sings, "Oh boy, Oh, joy, where do we go from here?"

No one knows.

A Bit of Gray in a Blue Sky: The Beautiful Story of the Bird That Saved the Lost Battalion

(*Ladies Home Journal*, August 1919)

This piece illustrates what would become a favorite technique of Lane's: picking an unusual character in her story through which the story could be told. This adherence to an absolute point of view would become one of her hallmarks. Here, Lane tells the true story of a homing pigeon that saved the lives of an American battalion cut off behind enemy lines in Europe when it managed to fly through gunfire to deliver a message giving the soldiers' position. The short factual report here becomes a haunting metaphor for soldiers at war; it is told mainly from the point of view of the pigeon, Cher Ami.

He woke every morning before the sun lifted its rim above the roof tops of Paris and gilded their edges with its first pale gold. His round, bright eyes looked though grayness at his world, and he knew that it was good. Little nestling sounds were all about him; there was the first flutter of wings and the low, throaty murmuring, now here, now there, swelling and blending into the deep vibrating cooing of his many neighbors. He stretched a long, unfolding wing. The silver-gray feathers spread like a great fan, then snapped together again and settled against his side. His own throat swelled and became musical.

Then the sunlight came. It filled the air with happiness. From all sides rose the whirring of eager wings, and his own wings spread and carried him swiftly up into the warm blueness. The air flowed past him like water, rippling against his downy sides, pouring along the straight red legs. His smooth breast rested upon it as he rose and rose, circling, swooping, curving in and out among his neighbors.

The roof tops of Paris were small beneath him. White little clouds were his companions. Around and over him was the vast blueness of the sky, stirring with impulses that he knew, alive with familiar meanings. Life was his; life beat warmly within the soft feathers that shut it from the cold high air, and he knew that life was good.

Curving, swooping, circling and circling again, he came home. He came home to his own roof top, his one roof top among all the roofs of Paris. His claws were again on the edge of the eaves, and his folded wings touched the wings of his friends. Their throaty murmuring filled the air; the sun was warm on their backs. Water gleamed as it always had, in the stone trough in the courtyard, and there was food in the boxes. Strange and mysterious were the hands that placed the water and the food; purposes he could not know governed them. They came from another world, a world that did not concern him, a world that for him was not.

Water gleamed in the stone trough, and innumerable wings fluttered over it. His own wings fluttered in the water. Oh, the coolness of cool water against his skin, beneath the soft feathers! Sparkling drops flickered above him as he beat his wings in ecstasy.

He rose, and his claws curved again on the edge of the eaves. He ruffled his feathers; they stood upright, warm in the sun. Carefully, one by one, he smoothed and straightened them. Then his throat swelled again, and he murmured aloud to the sun and the wind his happiness and content. This was his life. He knew no other. He dreamed of no world that was not made of long silver feathers, of iridescent gleams, of sunlight and blueness and water and grain.

Beneath the roof tops of Paris there were blackness and despair. The fields of France were tortured by war; on a battle line that circled half the world men were killing each other. The cities of America were filled with the sound of marching feet.

The great machinery of human living was turned to human destruction. Women by millions had gone out of their shattered homes. Factories and shipyards blazed all night against dark skies. Huge buildings by thousands were rising to the clang of hurrying hammers. Administrative organizations that covered the globe were being created out of chaos. Somewhere among vast masses of papers there was a line of ink on a white page: "Carrier pigeon 43678; Cher Ami. Pigeon Division Number One; U.S.A. Signal Corps; 77th Div'n U.S. Inf., A.E.F."

These were words. And words were nothing to Cher Ami (Dear Friend). Man might dream of the celestial music of the stars in their courses, but he did not dream that men spoke to each other with words. His world was sunlight and feathers, the coolness of water, the roundness of grain golden and tempting, the blueness of skies, the swiftness of wings, home and his own roof top. These things he felt and knew; they were his life, and life was good.

Into this life of his, then, there came a vast purpose beyond the rim of things known, and it seized upon him and carried him away. He was in a box, a narrow space in which he could barely stretch his idle wings, and all the world was a jolting and a noise. When at last the box opened he was in a strange country. He sat on a roof top that was not a roof top. It was small and flat, it crawled over the ground on wheels, and his box was in it, and the boxes of his unhappy companions. They sat together, with heavy wings, and looked at a sky that was filled with sudden black clouds and bursts of white sound. Something called to them, saying "Come home!" but they could not rise and go. Never again would he see the happy roof tops of Paris.

But something else came to him that wiped away their memory. Out of the unknown again, it came and cooed beside him. The vast purpose he did not know had given him a mate. From all the strange birds that came to this roof top that was not a roof top, he chose her in a free and happy choice. She was his now as long as he should live, for that is the way of mating in his world. She was small and gray and gentle. She cooed beside him, and he did not hear again the voice that said "Come home!" He was at home!

When he was free again, they circled together in the golden blueness as the sun rose. They came together to the troughs where the grain was, and again water was provided for them, and they bathed in the sunlight. In their box appeared a bowl, a beautiful round bowl in which to build a nest. With gentle blows and scoldings in his throat he drove her to it. He would not let her stay away from it, for there were eggs in the nest. He felt the whiteness and the warm roundness of eggs; his soul was passionately concerned with them.

The roads of France were brown with marching ranks of soldiers in khaki. Great transport docks were being built upon the French shores. Airplanes filled the sky. Camps rose on land that had been orchards. Generals conferred in Paris. The air thrilled with invisible electric messages.

Cher Ami's mate sat upon her nest, and all his world was beneath her folded wings. Torn from her and carried far away, he sped back to her, panting. He brought her food. He watched her jealously when she stirred. He hurried her back when she paused too long on the edge of the bathing trough. And then there came a day when there were small birds in the nest. The crackle of shrapnel and the whir of airplanes were nothing to him then. He did not hear them. He did not know that they existed.

On the morning of October second orders came from the headquarters of the Seventy-seventh Division of Infantry, A.E.F., commanding the entire divisional line to advance to the La Viergette-Moulin de Charlevaux road and the railroad paralleling it. The object was to be gained "without regard to losses and without regard to the exposed condition of the flanks." Complying with these orders, the advance began about midnight.

Cher Ami was seized in the darkness. Horror and agony descended upon him, without purpose or meaning. His little gray mate, his nest, the core of his life was gone. His wings struck implacable barriers. The night was a roar and a blackness, shot with intolerable flashes of light. Into the Argonne woods, under the merciless fire of the Germans, thousands of men were marching in the dark, and he went with them.

Under the torn trees, tangled in barbed wire, mangled by machine-gun fire, the troops went forward. And dawn and day and evening again came to a heartbroken bird in a basket, beating against the inexorable bars that kept him from his gentle mate and his nest.

At dusk that night the Americans went down a slope, crossed a stream, and stopped on the steep side of a hill, just under the road they had been sent to reach. They had fought for eighteen hours under ceaseless fire, through a wood filled with machine-gun nests and barbed-wire entanglements, and over a system of German trenches. A hundred men lay dead behind them. Runners carried back to headquarters the message: "The objective has been reached." And the men rested.

On the map at headquarters General Alexander marked their position. On the right, the 154th Brigade had been stopped. On the left, the line held its own place. In the center, the First Battalion of the 308th Infantry and part of the Second Battalion had broken through, and lay unsupported on either side, having won to the advance line as they had been ordered to do. The orders contemplated that the remainder of the line, advancing on each side, would reorganize, consolidate its position and prepare for a further advance.

Four hundred and eighty men, therefore, dropped where they stood, and slept. Their line of communication was established to the rear. Their position, on the precipitous side of the hill, protected by thickets and bowlders [*sic*], furnished with water from the stream in the valley, was good. They lay there and slept, dead to the roar of the guns.

And Cher Ami in his basket lay with them.

At daybreak the officers heard commands from the wood behind them, commands spoken in German! A patrol was sent back along the line of communication. It found that the men who had been posted in the rear were dead, and the line broken. A hundred and fifty men were then sent out to break through the German lines, join their comrades in the rear, and attack with them. Of these men, eighteen got through to the south, and a platoon returned to the battalion.

The Germans in the night had closed in behind the peak of the advance line, cutting it off and completely surrounding the Americans.

The men were not greatly alarmed. Each man dug himself in on the steep clay bank, looked to his ammunition, and prepared to hold the hill until the line advanced on either side and wiped out the enemy behind. But the line did not advance. The sun rose on a day torn by the rattling crackle of machine guns raking the hill. The solid earth spouted geysers of dust under showers of hand grenades. At noon began the ceaseless, shattering roar of the trench mortars, and the air became a torturing chaos of sound.

Beyond the forest smashing artillery fire heralded the attacks of rescuers. Five times the attack was launched, and each time beaten back. Still embedded within the stubborn German lines more than four hundred men clung to the side of the hill and fought desperately under an incessant crossfire. So the first day and the first night passed.

And in his basket Cher Ami lay palpitating and sick with uncomprehended horror.

The second day found the men with little ammunition and no food. The nerve-breaking roar had not for a second abated. The hill was torn to pieces. The stream in the valley was battered into a morass. In the shell holes, wounded men lay and moaned for water. Cher Ami, in his basket, watched his four companions depart, one by one, rising into the smoke darkened air, circling and disappearing.

At headquarters no word came from the Lost Battalion. General Alexander, ordering attacks toward its position, dispatched airplanes to search for it from the sky. Two planes were shot down. The others, circling above smoke clouds and thickets of underbrush, brought back no information. On the hill the men who were left tightened their belts, smiled grimly at Major Whittlesey's encouragement, and fought. At night the Germans attacked in force. The Americans held the hill. Toward dawn they buried their dead.

The third day many of the men were delirious for want of water. Runners were sent to the springs to fill canteens. The runners died. German machine guns covered the springs. The hollow where the stream had been was a marsh. Men crawled to it and sucked handfuls of the mud. They gathered the liquid ooze in cups and waited hours for it to settle that the wounded might drink.

The third night the Germans attacked again. But the Americans held the hill. The fourth morning found the men eating berries, leaves and bark. Airplanes, flying overhead in storms of bullets, dropped packages of food, but they fell in the woods where the Germans were.

Men rose from the shallow holes that were their only protection and waved signal flags, but the airmen did not see them. The Germans did. The men fell.

That day an American, desperately searching for one of the dropped packages, was captured by the Germans. He returned that afternoon bearing a message asking for surrender. Major Whittlesey read the letter slowly. Then he turned to Sergeant-Major Baldwin. "Take in the airplane signals," he said. They were white, and it might be that the enemy would think they meant surrender.

Over the rent and broken earth that had been a hill the air did not cease to shudder and crash with the roar of German guns. In the pits men bound the wounds of their comrades with strips of underclothing, leggings, string. Dead and living were flung together by the earth-exploding shells.

Upon this scene, then, there began to fall a steady, even, rapid shell fire from beyond the German lines. The guns of the French were trained on the hill. For five days no word had come from the Lost Battalion. All attempts to reach it had failed. The French, therefore, sure that it had been wiped out or had surrendered, were shelling its position, against the protests of General Alexander. The tortured men remaining were being killed by their own guns.

It was then that a blackened hand came into Cher Ami's basket and fastened to his left leg a strange thing, long and gray and hard. For five days he had lived without food or water. Now he was seized again and flung upward into smoke and fire and shrieking things.

Flung upward, but into stinging, blinding pain. For hardly had his wings taken hold of the air when agony struck him, stopped him, pierced him through and through. He fluttered and fell, fluttered, caught at the air and reeled. "God!" said the haggard man in the shell hole below. "He's done for."

Convulsively the strong wings struck out again. Then they steadied and held the air. Cher Ami wavered, rose and wavered again. Then he vanished above the smoke. There was clear air around him. Beneath him was such a world as he had never seen, a hideous world without meaning or purpose. Only his wings were the wings he had known, and they carried him around and around, in weary circles.

As he circled he heard a silent voice, a voice without words, that said: "Come!" "Come!" said the wordless message. "This is the right way. Follow it. Come!"

Without knowing how he knew, and without questioning, he followed the call through the trackless air. His wings carried him up, stroke by painful stroke, against the strong invisible current. Past the smoke and the roar, past blurring green fields and curling, moving lines of tan, over and beyond into a strange country he went, a throb of pain that answered a voiceless call.

There was water there below him, but he did not stop. There would have been grain, perhaps, in the fields, but he did not think of it. He went on till his eyes were blind and his sobbing heart ached in his aching breast.

Forty miles from the spot where the Lost Battalion, crazed but fighting, was dying under the guns of both friend and foe, Sergeant Kochler at headquarters in Rampont saw a handful of bloody feathers drop from the sky. It struck breast first that roof top which was not a roof top. It fluttered a second, came reeling on one bleeding leg, and hopped blindly toward that landing board beyond which had been a nest.

Sergeant Kochler lifted a gaunt and quivering little body in his hands. Dangling still on the ligaments of a leg that had been shot away was the aluminum message carrier. Inside was the first message that had come from the Lost Battalion. It recorded position and situation, and said, "Your barrage is falling on us. For God's sake, stop it!"

The barrage was stopped. That night the 307th Infantry broke through the German lines to the hill, and a hundred and ninety-four men, all that was left of the Lost Battalion, staggered or were carried to safety.

Cher Ami, doomed never again to grip with two firm red feet the happy eaves of Paris, lay bandaged and helpless beneath the incomprehensible hands that had shaped his life.

And now he lives again in his own world, a world of long silver-gray feathers of iridescent gleams, of sunlight and blueness and water and grain, a world whose core and meaning is the gentle mate and the fledglings in the beautiful brown bowl.

Cher Ami is carried sometimes, for unknown reasons, in a cage, and on the cage there will soon be something that sparkles. It will be a Distinguished Service Cross, the only bird to receive such an honor, presented to him because, wounded, he saved the lives of one hundred and ninety-four American soldiers. But to him it is only a sparkle.

In his world there are no generals, no soldiers, no great struggles of mankind toward a light that leads them. He does not know what vast and mysterious purposes may lie beyond his imagining. He does not know what he did, nor why. For he, like a man or a star, lives in a universe shut in by walls of the things he knows.

3.
Mrs. Lane Writes for the Red Cross

After World War I, Lane's work with the Red Cross Publicity Bureau led her to write about conditions for women and children in Europe and the United States. She approached this work from her own position as a woman, and the pieces included here offer a glimpse into her conversational reporting style. They also continue to reflect a focus on a particular point of view, often her own, through which a story is told. This technique helped her writing grow beyond the retelling of facts to the construction of literary form in her work, and laid a foundation for her later fiction storytelling. Lane was finally able to go to Europe as the teens drew to a close, and she joined a Parisian literary scene that included a number of American expatriates, including Dorothy Thompson, who would become a lifelong friend.

She wrote a San Francisco neighbor and friend, Berta Hader, from Paris in September 1920: "I work along; two stories in Good Housekeeping, *three translations of Bernhardt for Betty [Beatty, editor of* McCalls*]; endless vistas of unwritten copy before me like the catacombs before the driven . . ." And yet, generating income was apparently a real concern for Lane during this period as well. Another letter to Hader explained why Lane could not continue a drawing class she had thoroughly enjoyed while in Paris: "I am so broke that I must write and write and write and can not*

waste the days of my middleage in riotous happiness in a drawing class," she wrote.*[1] *The mandate that she tell her stories "from the women's perspective" meant that much of her published material focused on maternal and child issues. The two pieces in this section demonstrate the areas of concern Lane reported about for the largely female audience of* Good Housekeeping. *Written under the auspices of the Red Cross Publicity Bureau, each sought to shed light on a particular social issue that was placed within the sphere of domesticity thought to appeal to women.

The Children's Crusade

(*Good Housekeeping,* November 1920)

"The Children's Crusade" details the struggles of European children and families to pick up the pieces after the Great War was over. Lane specifically focuses on the roles of American and European children in helping with the recovery efforts. In the story, readers can see Lane's commitment to telling a story from her particular point of view, as well as her ability to provide the vivid description and dialogic details that make her readers a part of the conversation that Lane is having with her subjects. The story also demonstrates Lane's ability to take a simple assignment—reporting about how American children were helping European children through the Red Cross—and turn it into literary art.

In the houses on that pleasant American street, it was not necessary to look at the clock to know that it was noon. The voices of the children announced it in a burst of joyous clamor, when the open school doors poured them out upon the sidewalks. For the moment the other business of the street disappeared before them; their coming was like an invasion from another world, for what can we really know of that intense and passionately interesting life bounded by the school walls, preoccupied with lessons, recitations, notes slipped from hand to hand, interlacings of secret glances, rivalries, friendships, all in an atmosphere of chalk-dust and erasers whispering on blackboards? These little beings that are the very core of our lives have a life of their own now, filled with its own facts and

1. RWL to Berta Hader, September 7, 1920, RWLP, box 5, file 64; RWL to Berta Hader, November 30, 1920, RWLP, box 5, file 64.

dreams. Out of it they burst upon us abruptly with surprises, with requests and statements logical to them and amazing to us; for the things that are important to us have not meaning for them, and the great matters that absorb them fill us with hidden laughter.

The sound of the children's voices in the street was a signal to my hostess. She lifted the lid of the little oven on the gas burner to test the baking potatoes, and opened the ice-box. I sliced bread while she filled the glasses with milk, and in a moment, with a banging of doors and a clatter in the hall, the children were there. Rosy, happy, bursting with all the news of the morning, they climbed into chairs and seized knives and forks, and the business of eating proceeded in that distracted incoherence that children always bring to a table.

"But, dear, perhaps he was mistaken. I'm sure his mother wouldn't— No, Helen, eat all your potato, first. Dear, please don't hold your knife that way. I think I put the whistle on the shelf in the hall closet. Are you sure the teacher wants you to bring it?—Bobby, you really mustn't take such big mouthfuls—"

Through this customary confusion a request cut its way suddenly.

"Mama, give me a quarter?"

"Yes, mama, I want one, too!"

"So do I!"

It was one of the tiny crises that filled their mother's busy, homemaking days. There are so many ways to spend seventy-five cents. And there were still bills for the new school clothes and books, shoes were already scuffed out at the toes, tablets and pencils and hair-ribbons must be bought, Christmas was coming.

How could the children know what arguments would move the incomprehensible adult mind? They knew only that it was infinitely important that they have that money. They could do nothing without her assistance; they were helpless, but valiant. "Everybody's going to take a quarter," they said. And, "It's for poor children in France and places." Then with an air of finality they pronounced the name of a great organization to which, for four years, Americans had given with lavish hands. Their mother sighed.

"Well, bring me my purse. It's in the top bureau drawer."

They kissed her, warmly and shyly, and started away with a heedless rapidity that disturbed the hall rugs, and were called back to put on their rubbers, and were gone, leaving the nervous house to settle into quietness again.

While we washed the dishes their mother said thoughtfully: "I suppose we should be glad to have enough to eat and wear—of course when you think of the children in Europe—but surely there ought to be some way for Europe to begin taking care of them by this time. I don't want to be selfish, but after all we have our own to think of, and it seems to me I've done nothing for four years but give and give."

Thinking of our own American children in slums and factories, of our thousands of babies dying for want of food and care, of the ignorance, malnutrition, and disease in our own country, her feeling seemed justified. It has taken eight thousand miles of travel by land and sea and a thousand years of going backward into primitive conditions of living to show me how wrong we were in this attitude. I am humble about it, for it seems to me now that the children knew. It seems to me that they understood, somewhere in that secrecy of children's souls to which we never quite penetrate, that they were not offering a day's charity to a day's hunger, but that they were embarking upon a great adventure in living, I think that the fourteen million of them in America know, as the children of France, Italy, Austria, Bohemia, Moravia, and Montenegro know, that they are beginning again, in terms of the twentieth century, a Children's Crusade toward a better world than we have given them.

In every country the movement has its shepherds who have seen a vision, but it is the faith of the children that is making it a movement history will record when the great war has become a date to be memorized. Children are so weak, so dependent, so charmingly funny in their first startled encounters with facts, that even when we love them we do not consider them seriously, as we consider parliaments or armies. They grow up around our feet as saplings grow in a forest. But tomorrow they will be the forest. In thirty years the children will be the world, they will be its parliaments and armies; and today they are uniting, across barriers of frontiers and races and religions, in a movement to make that world united and peaceful.

They are meeting on the one fundamental human basis, for the one experience common to all human beings is the experience of being a child in an unknown world; and they are saying to each other: "Let us begin our investigation of this strange planet by knowing that we are friends. That is the first fact. And the second fact is that we are all alike. We all want to be happy and good, each in our own way; we all want to be loved and to play and to learn and to taste the curious flavors of living, to climb mountains and measure stars and watch the ways of insects and animals and plants. We like the same fairy tales, dream the same dreams, and feel the same pains. If there are quarrels between us, they are only little quarrels that we shall soon forget, for we have begun by playing together and picking each other up when we fall, and we shall go on to studying and working together. We are really friends and always shall be."

They do not say these things with words; children need not trouble with the clumsiness of words, for their clear feelings are not yet obscured by the complexities of thinking. But this is the spirit in which, from the red-gabled houses of France, from the olive groves of Italy, from the shadow of medieval castle walls in Austria, the low, white villages of Czecho-Slovakia, and the windowless stone huts of Montenegro, the children are rising to join the children of America, as their spirit marches eastward across Europe. There is something in this too big to be written. There is a hope in it that flutters and grows faint when it encounters the harsh realities we know. We have learned too much since the thirteenth century to believe that children can redeem the sins of the world. One must be a child again to believe that. But the children do believe it—these children who will take that belief with them into tomorrow. They believe it because they do not know these hard realities that, after all, vanish like smoke with each generation's passing; they believe it because they are already beginning to create the world around them in the image of the new realities that American children are showing them.

The movement began, as so many ventures of children do begin, in their eagerness to emulate us. There was the big Red Cross to which we were busy supporting our men in the war by trying to undo what war did to them, and there followed the Junior Red Cross, organized to help us. For twelve months the children rolled bandages, made field-dressings, collected tin-foil, learned to knit, manufactured with their little hands fifteen million articles for the soldiers. Their enthusiasm overran all efforts to hold it in sedate regulations. There was nothing they could not contrive to do. In Southern California they earned money by killing gophers; in Texas they organized Pig Clubs and raised pork to help the Food Administration; in Idaho they scoured the sage-brush plains, collecting bits of wool where sheep had rubbed their backs, until they had five hundred pounds of wool to be knitted into sweaters. Then the war ended, and in the sob of relief that went up from the world there was a little gasp of dismay from the children. What should they do next?

There were many consultations in the big white marble building in Washington. The parent organization, following its policy of diverting its activities from war abroad to peace at home, sought to turn the energy of the children back upon themselves. The Health Game was started in American schools, and fourteen million children who wore the little red cross diligently brushed their teeth, washed their faces, slept with open windows, resisted pickles and candy, and breathed deeply. But already their interests and activities were wider than America; in the Philippines 100,000 children had joined them; in Shanghai 25,000 young Chinese had come into the family. Also, they owned property in France and Belgium and on the seas; the ten million dollars they had amassed was not all spent. And already their leaders had seen a vision.

Diplomats at Versailles were still discussing new boundary lines when the children of America set out to carry across all frontiers the message of the brotherhood of the world's children. There were gifts in their hands, but their spirit was not that of that charity. It was a spirit of common fellowship, and it is not gratitude alone, but something finer and more enduring that one finds wherever they have passed.

Eight months after the first messenger from America's children had gone that way, I went down the white road that leads from the little hill-town of St. Francis of Assisi to Perugia, another old town upon the Umbrian hills. It is a long way from the pleasant American street where at that moment the children were sleeping, a long way measured not only by leagues, but by centuries. For even the name of these hills recalls the time, four thousand years ago, when men of the Iron Age came down over the Alps into a central Italy still shaken by the cataclysm that separated Sicily from the mainland. "Ombrixei," they were named by the Greek tribes in the Balkans, meaning, "men who fear the invasion of waters." To the peasants who trudged behind little ox-drawn plows on the golden-brown hillsides, and to the peasant women with baskets balanced on their yellow-kerchiefed heads, the old Roman road was a modern improvement, for in their veins is still the blood of the men who took these fertile lands while the sea was yet retreating from the Umbrian hills. They took these lands and tilled them, and held them upon Italy in the centuries while mankind was roving over a hemisphere still being made by earthquake and volcanic upheaval. And in the chatter of the soft-eyed children, who came running to crowd around me in the little town of St. Francis, there remain traces of the language spoken four thousand years ago by "the men who feared the invasion of waters."

"You are American?" they asked shyly, as we walked across the rough-hewn cobbles St. Francis had trod, and went into the little church where his deeds are recorded in paint on the walls. "See," they said, pointing to the pictures that showed the gentle saint scolding the wolf for his fierceness, talking to the birds, giving his cloak to a beggar, "He is our St. Francis, who loved all sad people and was good to them, like the Americans." It was a faith that made one humble, and a little ashamed.

So I went down the white road toward the old Franciscan hospital where St. Francis, brown-robed and bare-footed, went every day to tend the lepers. Alone among brown fields and leafless tree-trunks wreathed with grapevines there was the long building of age-yellowed gray stone. And in the field beside it a riotous crowd of Italian boys was playing football.

They did not stop playing because an observer stood astounded at the edge of the field. The struggle went on, panting and fierce, directed by breathless yells, until the shout that rose from a tangled mass of legs and arms showed that some one had scored. Then one might diffidently approach and cautiously [begin] to break down the wall of reticence behind which all half-grown boys retreat. From what miraculous skies did a football drop upon the Umbrian hills? From America, they said, and the word loosed an avalanche of questions.

"You know Detroit?" "You know Chicago?" "You have seen Kansas?"

"Why do you ask about Detroit?"

The questioner did not reply, turning aside his brown eyes and digging a toe into the ground. The answer came from others:

"He has a friend in Detroit."

"A friend? From here?"

"An American friend. He writes to him. I have a friend in Philadelphia. I have a friend in California, too. He went there from Philadelphia. It is three thousand miles. America is a big country."

The old Franciscan monastery is now a school—the delicacy of the Italians will not call it an orphanage—for boys whose families were murdered by the war. Thirty years ago, an Italian Jew, Levy Morenus, founded it upon a saying of Benjamin Franklin, who, lending money to someone in need, said, "I am too poor to give this to you. When you can, repay it by lending it to some one else, and tell him to repay you by passing it on to another who needs it." For thirty years the school and its farms were maintained by this spirit of cooperation, the orphans working in the fields making money to support more orphans, so that each boy held his head high, feeling himself not an object of charity, but a unit in a society that was self-reliant. The war would have destroyed this shelter for its victims, had not the American children offered to help support it; and the Italian boys took the help in the same spirit in which they help others. Are they not all children, helping each other? The Americans have come into the family, that is all. They are now part of the Italian *cooperativa* as they are becoming part of the legend of St. Francis. And the Italian boys welcome the newcomers as boys welcome a new and interesting schoolmate.

"Do our American friends train the vines so?" they asked, showing the dead tree trunks on which the vines were carefully festooned.

"And how do they make soap?" they wanted to know, when one of them dropped his hoe to stir the boiling kettle of fat and lye. For on that school farm, managed by the boys themselves, neither material nor time is wasted. Fifteen older boys apportion the tasks each month, send this group to care for the rabbits, that one to tend the vines, these boys to keep the bedrooms clean, those to do the kitchen work. School follows them to the fields, the master giving out arithmetic problems while the hoes are busy. "If ten of your cabbages die, Gino, at what price must you sell the others to make a profit?" And when Gino hesitates, "You will make no profit, Gino, if you can not answer that."

The profit is important, for it is Gino's contribution toward bringing another orphan into the school. Every month the *cooperativa* meets around the scrubbed, old, wooden table in the stone-floored kitchen-dining-room, and here, with the shining copper cooking pots on the walls around them, the boys settle the problems of the Collestrada colony and solemnly debate the election to the *cooperativa* of newcomers still on probation.

"Is this the way it is done in your country?" the president asks when the meeting has adjourned, for he would be willing to learn better methods of presiding at a *cooperativa* meeting. You compliment his skillful leadership, while some of the boys stretch a white cloth on the walls, and others watch the proud manipulator of the magic lantern that has come from the American children. The boys not yet admitted to the *cooperativa* crowd through the doorways and bring in benches. The excitement is so great that they can hardly settle into silence, for they are about to see a magic lantern show. Marvelous invention from marvelous America!

"Will you say to our American friends that we thank them for the magic lantern and for the football?" The English names sound strange in the midst of the soft Italian. "A baseball has come, also, but we do not yet know how to use it. What is it, a first base?"

You share your meager knowledge of baseball. The scuffling rows of boys are still now, and the first shining colored picture slides through the darkness. Brooklyn Bridge! They recognize it with excited exclamations.

Outside on the old white Roman road a peasant's cart lumbers past, drawn by two plodding oxen. From the door-step one sees the dark masses of olive trees, and the straggling lines of the vineyards. Here and there a light moves uncertainly, a torch carried in a dark village street. Over the low line of the hills the old stars swing again, the stars that saw the tribes of the first Ombrixei, the wars of the Iron and Bronze ages, the conquests of the Gauls and the camp-fires of Hannibal's army; the stars that are looking down now upon a new thing, the first effort at understanding and friendship among the children of the world.

Beyond the Alps lies Italy's ancient enemy, Austria, the nation that inherited, five hundred years ago, the fear and hate that the peoples of Italy have felt for the danger from the north ever since the sea retreated from the Umbrian hills. Austria, crushed and ground under the heel of Italy at last, hating Italy with a hate poisoned by helplessness, and hated in turn with the cruelty added to anger by fear.

All the world has heard of Austria's suffering; no one really knows it who has not seen it. But among these people whose bodies have been drained of red blood by slow starvation, these men who have lived on husks and turnips, in rooms unheated through the winter, these women whose husbands have been killed, whose sisters and children have died, there is only one answer to the hope of a world without war. I heard it in the huge hotels on The Ring in Vienna, in the government offices that are now in the old city palace of the Hapsburgs, on the terraces of the middle-class cafes, among the thousands that crowded St. Stephen's Cathedral to hear mass beneath the ancient Gothic arches and the jeweled light of stained-glass windows.

"Yes, the war is terrible. We have suffered more than we thought we could endure and live. But—you mean a future without war? That can never be for Austria. We have too many enemies."

They did not say it with pride or hatred, they said it hopelessly; but they said and believed it. The most heart-sickening fact in the dying city was that not even their experience of war could make them refuse to accept it as a necessary part of life.

There was only one flickering spark in the midnight of Vienna, and that was in the hospital wards where the children were. For four years the doctors and nurses had fought with bare hands against a rising flood of diseases from malnutrition. Their medicines had run low, their instruments had worn out, there had been no soap, no disinfectants, no sheets to replace old ones, nothing with which to make bandages and dressings. The children lay in beds whose linen was patches of old cloth, their pillow-cases gray and falling to pieces, their mattresses mended with many-colored twine. But the bandages and dressings were new and soft and white. They had been made by the children of America—made in American schoolrooms for the wounds of American soldiers, and given now the war was over, to soothe the pain of Austrian children. And the Austrian children knew it. They smiled from the pillows, they waved their hands, and their friendly eyes followed our progress between the rows of beds while a little murmur ran behind us, *"Americanische!"*

When I came out of the Kinderklinac there was a long line of women waiting for the street-car. They had been waiting for hours at the clinic, there were sick babies and crippled children in their arms, and there were far too many of them to get in one of the crowded cars. So, in the patient Austrian way, they had formed a line and stood waiting their turn. I would have taken my place in the line, but a murmur arose, and hands pushed me forward, while heads nodded encouragingly.

"Americanische! Americanische!" they said, smiling, trying to make me understand.

"You go first," said a woman who knew a few words of English. "American, yes? You go on, that's all right."

"But you're tired, and you have the baby. I can wait."

"No, no! You stand first. You don't wait. You are American. We like Americans."

"But why do you like Americans?" I exclaimed. "America fought you in the war. Perhaps you would have won the war if we had not fought. Perhaps the war would have ended two years sooner. I should think you would hate us."

"It is true, you fought us. But we like you. You have fed our children. And look—" she touched the dressings on the baby's arm.

"American children made these for us. No, you go first. We all say so."

A week later my train was running northward across the smiling land of Czecho-Slovakia. The pleasant country, green and rolling as the prairie lands of Iowa, was dotted with the darker green of pine forests and the bright colors of little groups of houses, long low houses with smooth white plaster walls and roofs done in patterns of red and white tiles. Many little streams arched with trees wandered across the meadows, and every stream had its flock of fat white geese tended by little barefoot girls in red and blue gowns. Men and women were working together in the hay-fields, and down the hard roads came carts woven of willow and drawn by little shaggy ponies, one in the shafts and one trotting beside them. And suddenly against the strange landscape appeared an American flag. It was on a flagpole, carefully carried up the road by a little boy in a short green jacket, red trousers, and bare legs. Where it was going I shall never know, or why. It appeared and vanished, a bit of home in that far country, a symbol borne by a child, and only many years can make its meaning clear.

It is a year since the first Junior Red Cross representative came into Prague, invited by the new government that drew so much of its inspiration from America. What could American children send to Bohemia, the nation whose firm hold on liberty has endured through five hundred years of oppression, the race that has given the world some of its greatest musicians and poets and reformers, the people whose culture is as old as Rome, whose cities and churches are the most beautiful in Europe, whose factories produce Bohemian glass, whose very sidewalks are works of art in mosaic? Miss Alice Masyrk, the president's daughter, answered the question quite simply.

Tooth-brushes! Bohemia could recover from the war, but not in time to save the children's teeth. Tooth-brushes cost twenty-five Bohemian crowns each, the equivalent, in Bohemian families, of five dollars in an American household. Would the American children send tooth-brushes to the Bohemian children?

The tooth-brushes came—not so many as were needed, but several thousand—and the Health Game was started in Czecho-Slovakia's schools. It was here that the Junior Red Cross made a mistake; it would not be human if it did not make mistakes. This was, after all, a natural error. It brought in the Health Game, exactly as it is played in America. The children heard its rules with excited interest. They were delighted to join the Americans in that strange game. The pupils in each school were divided into groups, ten under a lieutenant, fifty under a captain as in America, except that the titles were translated into terms of the military ranks of Czecho-Slovakia, and the game began. The tooth-brushes were distributed: booklets explained the importance of brushing the teeth, of sleeping with open windows. Then, unaccountably, enthusiasm flagged.

The children did not like to show their report cards. They did not seem happy to receive honors and promotions in rank. They brushed their teeth, and diligently bathed, and fought victorious battles with horrified mothers over the question of open windows at night, but something was wrong. They did not enjoy it. At last a teacher surprised the secret.

"Do American children like war?" The question came with that artless irrelevance that makes children the endless delights they are. The teacher was wise enough to follow this astonishing suggestion to its source without terrifying the questioner into the child's quail-like concealment. The whole, unhappy perplexity was laid before her. If American children did not like war, why did they play games with captains and lieutenants in them? Bohemian children did not like soldiers; they did not like to play they were soldiers. They liked to be healthy, but couldn't they, please, be healthy without being lieutenants and captains?

The change was not too difficult to make. Bohemian children were satisfied with a change from military to civil rank, and the school year of 1920 began with 100,000 Czecho-Slovakian children playing the Health Game in glad competition with America's fourteen million; while throughout Bohemia, Moravia, and Ruthenia boys and girls in gay peasant costumes whittle and paint fantastic wooden toys and labor over post-cards to be sent across the seas to America's schools. Bohemian children are stretching out their hands to meet those of America's children; there is no shyness between them. In a moment they will be showing each other their treasures, and there will be a friendship between them that will outlast childhood's forgotten toys.

But the crusade moves farther eastward to stranger lands—through the gondola-floating streets of Venice, on past many-colored Trieste, down the Dalmatian coast in a little steamer that lies every night moored in some shallow harbor because there are still dangerous mines in the Adriatic Sea, and at last into the stone-walled port of Cattaro beneath the four-thousand-foot height of Lovchen mountain. And up and over the mountain in a groaning automobile that astonishes the mountain goats, and down again into bleak Montenegro, a country that seems made of gray stones piled and scattered in some giant's idle moment.

The people that live in these mountains are strong, fierce and wild as their country, and their huts that rim the edges of the small bits of fertile land in the valleys seem part of the mountains themselves. Built of gray rocks, windowless, without chimneys, furniture, or any floor except the earth, they house the women who work the scanty fields, the men who have always gone to war, and the children—the children of Montenegro, half of them orphans.

It is a small light that the children of America carry into Montenegro, but the word of their coming goes over the highest mountain tops. The old house on a narrow, crooked street in Podgoritza had not recovered from its surprised encounter with American scrubbing brushes, when the children began to come, brothers and sisters carrying the smaller babies and managing somehow, without food or compass or companionship, to travel hundreds of miles to the Americans. All day long they banged upon the high wooden gate that shut the crazy rectangle of courtyard from the street, and the old gateman rose from his sheepskin and opened it to let in determined, upstanding youngsters clothed in rags and dirt, dying of fatigue and hunger, but valiant to the last.

How could one begin to count what Montenegro needed? The children's messenger had come from the twentieth century back into the dark, forgotten past of mankind. These are people who live by the most primitive agriculture, by herding goats and sheep in the mountains, and by war.

They have no schools, no commerce, no machinery. Montenegro has never heard of an invention so modern as a spinning-wheel. There are only the mountains and the people.

The first task was to take in the wandering children and feed and clothe them. It was not what the Junior Red Cross had hoped to do, but it must be done. The low, stone-walled rooms lining the courtyard of the house in Podgoritza were scrubbed to their gorgeously painted ceilings, beds were brought across three seas and a continent, an old stone trough was disinfected to make a bath-tub, and the children were let through the gates at which they knocked.

They liked to be washed. They ate like starving animals. But they stood astounded before the beds, not knowing what they were. They were amazed by sheets and pillows. And they moved silently about the courtyard, grave with the burden of their memories and the strangeness of the place. They sat in the sun and talked solemnly, while outside the gate the life of Podgoritza flowed through the narrow street—tall, fierce-eyed men in full blue trousers and red broadcloth coats heavy with gold embroidery, their purple sashes stuck through with silver-mounted revolvers and damaskeened knives, women with stone jars on their heads, tiny donkeys hidden under bundles of wood, milch goats driven from door to door. It was a torrent of strange and savage life, driving on in the course it had always taken. What could the children's crusade do against it?

It could only wash and feed a few children. It could only improvise wash-basins of blue pudding-dishes, and water-pitchers of a curiously discovered store of watering-pots, and show the children how American children wash their faces. It could only open its bright, new dining-room on the Fourth of July and lead the wide-eyed orphans to a table spread with a white cloth, set with plates and knives and forks, and decorated with sponge cakes supporting American flags. At that incredible sight the children cried aloud, "Hvalla-gospoditza!" meaning, "Thank you." And soon afterward they were singing their mountain songs in the courtyard. Before the summer ended, Montenegro's farthest mountain dweller wanted passionately to learn the American ways.

There is now a trade-school in the "eagle's nest of the world." At Donilovgrad, beneath the snow-covered heights of the Dinaric Alps, fifteen hundred Montenegran boys who read and write are learning there how to use tools. From the other side of the earth, from the other side of ten centuries of civilization, the American children are teaching them. Even Montenegro is falling into step with the children of the world.

It is too soon to say how far they will go, our children who are setting out toward a shrine we had almost abandoned. Their voices are lost in the noise of thirty wars that still soak our earth with blood. Their hands hold such frail things—post-cards, dolls, picture-books, and bits of money sent across the seas. But for the first time in all the world's sad history the children who will be men tomorrow are learning to love and understand each other. This is a true thing; it is a thing that the centuries will remember. I think it is the greatest hope we can hold today.

Mother No. 22,999

(*Good Housekeeping,* December 1920)

This piece, also written and sent from Europe, addressed the issue of American maternal health for Good Housekeeping *magazine. Maternal health was a significant discourse for* Good Housekeeping *during the period with which Lane was associated; it was viewed as a key social issue around which American women, who received the vote in 1920, could rally politically. Lane's story focuses on the high rate of maternal death in childbirth in the United States at the time it was written; it functions as a call to arms for change, drawing on the experiences of American women including, perhaps, her own, as Lane had lost her only biological child at birth. In the same issue in which Lane's article appeared, the editor of* Good Housekeeping, *William Frederick Bigelow, cited it in his editorial calling for support of the Sheppard-Towner Bill, which, among other things, provided federal money for maternal and infant health programs. The story offers a first look at Lane's forming political ideologies and at her persuasive abilities, which she would later use in enforcing her own political agenda through* Woman's Day *magazine. It is also a forceful slice-of-life story that sheds light on the disparate healthcare conditions women faced across the United States in the early part of the twentieth century.*

Ann Hamilton was an American woman, born of the old pioneer stock that fought its way across this continent a hundred years ago. She loved America, its traditions, its ideals and its promises for the future in which her children would have their part. She faced the hardships of life on the Montana prairies with the same courage that had carried her grandfather through the wilderness, and the first thing she hung on the walls of the sod shanty to which her husband took her was an American flag.

"We'll teach the children what it means when they're old enough to understand," she said. There were three children, Robert and David, the three-year-old twins, and Marian, eighteen months old.

The sod shanty was a dot on a vast, empty plain. The nearest neighbor was four miles away. Water must be hauled in barrels more than a mile, for there was not money enough to dig a well. But Ann Hamilton was hopeful, and thrifty and willing to work. Her husband had homesteaded a quarter section of good land, and they saw before them a time when it would be green fields and pastures feeding sleek cattle, when there would be a big barn and a new house and money enough to give the children the best schooling.

Ann Hamilton planted a garden and made it grow; she raised chickens; she helped build a sod barn. She kept the shanty clean, did the washing and ironing and cooking; she bathed and fed the children, made them underwear of flour-sacking, and told them fairy stories.

In three years the well was drilled, and Ann Hamilton was making butter from the milk of three cows. In two more years, with her help, the hard first struggle on the land would be over. Her husband did the work of two men that year, putting in forty acres of wheat because America needed wheat to win the war. That autumn Ann Hamilton was expecting their fourth child.

"I can't go away to a hospital," she said. "The children are too little to leave. There wouldn't be anyone to take care of them and the house and the butter-making."

So it was decided that she would stay at home. The doctor, twelve miles away, was notified to expect a summons, and a neighbor promised to come in and help for two or three days when the baby was born.

The pains began one night after the children had been put to bed. The husband hurried to catch and saddle a horse, and rode twenty-four miles to fetch the doctor. They reached the sod shanty at two o'clock in the morning. The neighbor had come, but she was not a trained nurse and did not know what to do. Ann Hamilton was in agony; evidently something was wrong.

The doctor did his best, but he was not a surgeon, and he had nothing with which to work. He attempted twice to use instruments, without success. When his patient had been in labor for two days and three nights, he saw that she must be taken to the nearest hospital. He sent for an automobile, put her into it and set out. They drove one hundred and fifteen miles over the rough roads of the Bad Lands. In the hospital Ann Hamilton gave birth to a stillbirth baby. The next day she died of exhaustion.

She died because she was an American woman. Had she been living in New Zealand, in Sweden, in any other nation except Spain and Switzerland, her country would have taken care better care of her than we did. Ann Hamilton's story is a true story. Every year in the United States sixteen thousand women die as she died, because they have not had the absolute necessities of care in childbirth.

Many times that number of babies dies from the same cause. One baby in every ten born in the United States dies before it is a year old—nearly a quarter of a million babies every year. Half of them die in the first six weeks after birth, chiefly from causes relating directly to improper care of the mother.

These figures are approximate, for we do not even count the births and deaths of American babies. Only twenty-three states enforce adequate laws for the registration of births. The lives of the babies, bought with the suffering every mother knows, flickers out in states too careless even to record their coming. The Children's Bureau of the United States Department of Labor, by making a house-to-house canvass of conditions in typical sections of this country, was able to arrive at this careful estimate of the numbers of babies that die in America because of neglect.

Great men in American life have denounced race-suicide in no uncertain terms. Press and pulpit have declared that the vitality of a nation, its power in war and its progress in peace, depend upon the willingness of women to bear and rear large families of healthy children. The responsibility and the blame of race-suicide have been placed on the shoulders of woman, and she has borne the blame as women have always borne the burdens, in silence. But has the responsibility been hers? Every year women endure a hundred thousand years of carrying the weight of unborn children, and their babies are born only to die before they have lived.

Nearly all these babies could be saved. They die from two causes, poverty and ignorance, and ignorance here is only another name for poverty, for the difference between the fortunate mother who has skilled medical attention and the mother who does not have it is rarely a difference of knowledge. It is a difference of income.

The poverty of an individual may be unavoidable; it may come upon him through no fault of his. Americans have never measured the worth of a man by his wealth, and it is a commonplace that the hardest, most necessary manual labor receives the smallest wage. But poverty of a community is always unnecessary; in this country it does not exist. The United States is the richest country in the world. It has millions for war, for foreign trade, for developing industry and agriculture, yet it lets one out of every ten of its babies die when money would save them.

Today, for the first time, the American woman shares the responsibility for their deaths. In our complex modern life it is only by community action that the natural rights of children can be restored to them; it is only through community care that all children can have an equal opportunity to be well-born of healthy mothers. The American woman is now a partner in the business of the community; it is she who must save the children.

"The government ought to do something about it," said one young North Carolina mother to the agent of the Children's Bureau. Her first baby, delivered by a midwife, had died when it was three days old. Remembering this, she sent her husband for a doctor on the eve of her second confinement. He was obliged to ride three miles and row across the river to reach the doctor's house; when he arrived the doctor was gone on another case. Meanwhile the mother had called a neighbor who sent for a midwife, but she was unable to handle the case properly. The mother had been in labor sixteen hours when the doctor came, and the baby was dead.

"Seems like we ought to have anyway one doctor in each township," the mother said.

Only five of the white families visited in that district lived within five miles of a doctor; more than one-fourth were ten miles or more from the nearest physician. Distance was not the only difficulty; in many cases the cost of the doctors' visit was prohibitive. Midwives charged only two or three dollars and helped the family somewhat with the nursing. None of the mothers had a trained nurse and only two had a "practical" nurse.

The care of the mothers consisted principally in large doses of tea made of catnip, tansy, sweet fennel, or wormwood. Two midwives advised giving the baby catnip tea; two, soothing syrup; two, whiskey; and four, paregoric. The windows were kept closed; one midwife considered it "against a woman to have too much air."

Three-fifths of all American babies are born in rural communities; these facts may be taken as typical, though perhaps extreme, examples of the conditions into which America welcomes her new-born citizens.

In the homesteading country studied in Montana less than one-fourth of the mothers had consulted a physician before confinement, and of these only three-fifths had seen him more than once. During the five years covered by the Children's Bureau survey eleven mothers died for every thousand births, and the minimum death-rate of babies less than five months old was 71 in every thousand.

These were children of American families—hardworking, intelligent, self-respecting people, the finest our nation produces. They died because their country did nothing to save them. Many miles from a doctor, too poor to pay for the expensive trip to a far-away hospital, the mothers did their best, and failed, and saw the baby laid in the little home-made box and carried by neighbors across the brown prairies to be buried.

"I got hold of the best doctor book I knew of, and we sat up most of the night reading it before the baby was born," they said. "I didn't feel right, but it's thirty-five miles to a doctor, and I couldn't leave the other children to go. The trip is so expensive, too; I didn't feel we could afford it."

These mothers are eager to learn how to care for themselves and their babies. They pass from hand to hand any printed scrap of information they can get. One woman, reading that cereals are good for babies, had gathered oats in her field, carefully husked the kernels, boiled them and fed them to her child. When the Bureau held a Children's Health Conference, families drove twenty-five miles and back in open wagons, and many came more than fifteen miles.

"The post-office is like a different place now on mail days," one woman said after the conference. "The mothers that come in, and the fathers, too, are asking each other what they feed the babies now, how the doctor's advice is working out."

"Since I took the baby off condensed milk and put her on cow's milk she gained a pound and a half," said another whose baby had been losing weight. "I've written all the mothers I know, telling them what a difference it's made."

There can be no doubt that that one conference, by giving information to prospective mothers about the care of themselves and their babies, has saved many lives. But it lasted only a week, and there is now no one in that county—an area larger than the state of Connecticut—to carry on the work. The county health officer, sixty-five miles away, is employed on a part-time basis, and his duties of inspecting meat-markets, dairies, and restaurants in the county seat make it impossible for him to go to other parts of the county. There are no public health nurses. In how many rural counties are there public health nurses?

Public health can be bought, if we will pay for it. England proved during the war that a nation can determine the death-rate of its babies. Mothers become valuable when men are dying in battle; it has been said that women can not bear arms, but they do bear soldiers. The war awakened European government to the fact that the constant waste of the lives of mothers and babies threatens the life of the nation, and European babies were safeguarded as never before. England enforced registration of all births within thirty-six hours, increased maternity and infant welfare work, doubled the number of public health nurses, and increased the number of welfare centers to 1276. In response to these efforts the infant mortality rate fell to the lowest point in England's history, a point much below ours.

It is not for war, but for peace, that America needs her children. For the building of her own future, for the happiness and prosperity of her people, for her honor among the nations, our country must stop this needless waste of her new life.

In 1916 more than 75,000 babies in the United States died before they were a month old. They died because their mothers were not given proper care and protection during the months of pregnancy. They died because we allowed pregnant women to be underfed or overworked, or both: because we let them struggle along without necessary medical and nursing care. In Waterbury, Connecticut, a typical Eastern manufacturing town, one mother dies for every 154 babies born; of the 2,144 live-born infants upon the survey was based, 263 died before they were a year old. These babies need not have died; whenever an attempt has been made to save the children, they have been saved.

In New York City a committee undertook a two-year experiment in prenatal work. It supervised, during pregnancy and for a month after their babies were born, nearly fifteen hundred women and gave them decent medical care. The proportion of their babies who died during the first month was nearly one-third less than in the city as a whole, and all but two of the mothers lived.

There is no escape from the conclusion that the United States, the richest nation in the world, is allowing every year a quarter of a million of her own children to be killed by poverty. All other causes come back, in the last analysis, to that one. It is poverty, in the rural districts, that makes doctors so inaccessible and drives mothers to facing the uncertainties of childbirth attended only by a midwife or a neighbor. It is poverty that leads, in the cities, to overwork, underfeeding, bad housing, and reliance on quack doctors.

"It is important to remember," says a Children's Bureau Bulletin, "that poverty lacks the defense against ignorance which is at the disposal of the well-to-do mother. Sir Arthur Newsholme says that the designation of maternal ignorance as the chief factor in child mortality is 'a comfortable doctrine for the well-to-do to adopt'; but he states that we have little reason for thinking that the ignorance of the working-class mother is much greater than that of mothers in other classes of society. The ignorance of the working-class mother is a menace because she is socially helpless unless the community will take the responsibility of providing adequate medical and nursing care, adequate teaching of maternity and infant hygiene, adequate provision for decent housing and sanitation, and adequate income for the father.

"The fathers of 88 percent of the babies included in the Children's Bureau studies earned less than $1,250; 27 percent earned less than $550. As the income doubled, the mortality rate was more than halved."

Let us be plain about this. We are Americans, proud of our country, proud of her traditions and her ideals, glad to feel that our allegiance is given to a great nation founded on the principles that all men are equally entitled to life, liberty, and the pursuit of happiness.

"We hold these truths to be self-evident; that all men are born free and equal—" Yet we face the fact that an American baby's right to life depends on the income of his father. Before he is born that decides his fate. The son of a well-to-do father has twice the chance to live that the son of the poor man has.

No democracy can survive when these things long continue to be true. The American ideal was not forever won when our forefathers won their struggle to make this country free; ideals must be rebuilt into reality every day if they are to endure. America must be made equally safe for all American babies, for democracy can exist nowhere if not in the cradle.

Investigation has shown that the babies of the poor, in cities and country, are dying for lack of necessary medical care of the mothers. It is clearly the duty of the community to provide such care, and experiments have provided such care, and experiments have proved that where it is given the babies live. England has proved it, New York City has proved it and New Zealand, with an excellent system of public health nurses and medical service, stands first among the nations on that list in which the United States stands eleventh.

Acting upon these facts, Miss Jeannette Rankin introduced into the Sixty-Fifth Congress of the United States a bill sponsored by Miss Julia Lathrop, Chief of the Children's Bureau, providing for a system Federal and State cooperation in caring for mothers and infants throughout America. The bill was introduced; it was referred to a committee for consideration; it was reported out of committee, referred to another one, and stopped there. Nothing was done.

There are many reasons for this. Washington is a place where all interests in America life converge; it is a huge governmental machine. Getting a bill through it is not a simple matter. Only one thing will do it, and that is a tremendous pressure behind the bill, an insistence that will not be denied, that does not for an instant relax, that grows in power and purpose until it wins.

The Maternity bill returned in the Sixty-Sixth Congress. Senator Sheppard, Democrat, introduced it in the Senate on October 20, 1910; it was labeled Senate Bill 3259, and referred to the Committee on Public Health, and National Quarantine. Representative Towner, Republican, introduced it in the House on December 5th; it became House Bill 10925, and was referred to the Committee on Interstate and Foreign Commerce. It will get no further until 1921 unless American women demand that it be passed.

Meanwhile in America a mother dies needlessly every thirty minutes, and the unnecessary deaths of five hundred babies a day are added to our shameful total.

The Maternity bill will create a system of caring for mothers and children that will be somewhat similar to the Farm Bureau system of caring for crops and live stock. The Federal government is authorized to appropriate $2,000,000 for the fiscal year ending June 30, 1921, to be apportioned among the states in proportion to their population and to be met by an equal appropriation from the state, the money to be spent in giving needed instruction and medical care to mothers and infants through public health nurses, consultation centers, and other suitable methods. The Annual appropriation from the state, the money to be spent in giving needed instruction and medical care to mothers and infants through public health nurses, consultation centers, and other suitable methods, is to be gradually increased to $4,000,000, in 1926. The work is to be under the direction of a Federal Board of Maternal and Infant Hygiene, consisting of the Secretary of Labor, the chief of the Children's Bureau, the Surgeon-General of the Public Health Service, and the United States Commissioner of Education.

Last year the Federal government spent $4,211,312 on the Bureau of Animal Industry; in the United States $10,087,240 was spent in cooperative agricultural extension work for the purpose of creating better farms, larger crops, and finer farm animals. Will the Federal government inaugurate in 1920 a similar system of caring for American mothers and babies?

It will not, unless the women of America demand it, and demand it in unmistakable terms. The millions of new women voters hold in their hands the power to decide. Let them demand that the bill be passed, let them put themselves on record as demanding it, let them make it clear that they will watch the record of every man in Congress on that question, and the work of saving America's babies will begin, and begin at once.

4.
Mrs. Lane Writes from Abroad

In Europe, Lane took advantage of the opportunity to travel to countries and places she had dreamed about. Some sense of her experiences shows through her Red Cross articles, but it is in the nonfiction pieces Lane wrote as travelogues that her sense of exhilaration and joy in her experiences comes through. Her forays into fiction writing had begun to prove profitable; a prize check for a short fiction story that won an O'Henry award in 1921 found her in Turkey. "Innocence," a dark story about culture clashes in the Florida backwoods, was loosely based on the Wilder family's sojourn in Florida years before, and it is told through the eyes of the little girl who witnesses it.

Its sale, and its winning of the prize, helped keep the wolf from the door for Lane, whose travel took her to what would become her favorite place in the world—Albania. Lane fell in love with Albania and Albanian culture, and in a short autobiography written for the Works Progress Administration in the thirties, claimed Albania as one of her two "hometowns." More of her travel writing has been published as Travels with Zenobia: Paris to Albania by Model T Ford, *an edited diary brought to publication by Roger Lea MacBride; and in Lane's own book about Albania,* Peaks of Shala, *first published in 1923.*

The two pieces in this section show the depth of that love for travel and for Albania and also show a slice of life from that early part of the twentieth century in the Near East and eastern Europe.

Budapest for a Bath

(*World Traveler,* May 1923)

This humorous vignette about a clash of cultures in a picturesque city captures the best of Lane's style: witty dialect and active description punctuate the short story of a moment in Budapest. It is a trivial moment that Lane turned into a masterpiece of storytelling that deftly illustrates the travails of traveling in the 1920s.

Several times we had been to Vienna, but we had never seen Budapest. Travelers don't, usually. Budapest is not far from Vienna, but the only city beyond it is Constantinople, and if you are going to Constantinople it's simpler to go through Belgrade on the Orient Express, or to take a boat from Trieste down the Adriatic and past the isles of Greece. After traveling for a time in Europe, one longs for simplicity in train schedules. But one also has another longing, and it was this which took us out of our way to Budapest. We wanted a bath.

In Vienna we had demanded a bath, and got it—for only 25,000 kronen a day. It was a large, beautifully tiled bathroom; we gloated over it. But we did not bathe in it. There was no hot water. Morning and evening, for large tips, servants brought a small lukewarm can of water to fill the washbowl, and this saved our self-respect. But abstinence made our hearts grow fonder when we remembered the baths of home.

"Are you going to Budapest?" friends said to us. "It's a fascinating city, quite Oriental." We said no, we were not going to Budapest.

"What do you mean—'Oriental?'" I asked suspiciously. For I had been assured that Warsaw was quite Oriental, and when I reached it I found that the only things to distinguish it from any American city were the few trees in the business streets. And I had been told that Cracow was very Eastern, and, except for the old, old castle where one can see the veritable bones of a dragon killed by one of Poland's first kings, it is not so Eastern as San Francisco's Chinatown.

"Budapest is very Oriental," our friends insisted, vaguely. And they mentioned suspension bridges across the Danube, and a castle built forty years ago in the style of centuries ago, and the first subway in the world, and the best modern hotel in Europe. "Quite Oriental," they repeated. "Oh, I don't know—it's the—the atmosphere. And then, of course, there are the baths."

"Baths!"

"Oh, yes, Oriental baths. Turkish baths. The Turks ruled Budapest for several centuries, you know. Marble baths, colored glass domes, swimming pools, masseuses—you know, the real Oriental baths. Dozens of 'em, dozens! You bathe like an Oriental lady—it's rather fun. That is, I never tried it myself, but—"

That night we counted the Mutual Fund and looked up the Hungarian exchange—750 kronen to the dollar—and next day promptly at one o'clock, as we had been instructed, we were at the station buying tickets for Budapest. They cost 20,000 kronen.

"You see," said the practical Peggy, closing the M.F. purse, "It's as cheap to travel in Europe as to stay anywhere you are. A day in New Bristol costs 25,000 kronen; a day on the train, only 40,000. And think what we save by not being able to shop!"

There seemed, somehow, to be something wrong with that reasoning. I said so, and as soon as we were settled in our compartment we went over the M.F. account-book with care. You may not believe it, but we had traveled for six months all through Europe, for less than it would have cost us to live at home. Cheered by this, we got out of the train and walked up and down the platform for some time, gazing out at baffled unhappy travelers on the other side of the gates—for the gates are closed at one forty, for some unknown reason, and neither prayer nor persuasion can get anyone past them after that. At two o'clock we got back into the compartment, and not much later departed for Budapest.

It was a pleasant little journey, through the softly green countryside of May. The Danube followed us, flowing wide and serene beside the tracks, though not even the blueness of the spring sky could make that river blue. We have been waltzing, so to speak, under false pretenses; beautiful the Danube is, but never blue. It is the noncommittal color of a mirror, and as a mirror it is most satisfactory, reflecting straight young trunks of beech trees, rushy green islands, curves of rolling flowery meadows, and many white streamers like large mechanical swans, that go up and down it all summer long.

At seven o'clock we arrived in Budapest, nicely in time to dress for dinner at the Ritz, that most modern and excellent of large hotels, which the Hungarians call the Duna Palota, or Danube Palace. From the windows of our large room we looked across the river at the Eighteenth-Century-style palace on the Often hill, and I said "Oriental!" in a vindictive tone. "I will bet you a new hat," said I, "that this city is as Oriental as a ham sandwich. I will bet the spiffiest hat in Budapest," said I, "that you can't find one trace of the Orient between now and tea-time tomorrow."

"Done!" said Peggy.

The hat was mine when we left the hotel at nine o'clock next morning; at nine-fifteen it was Peggy's. For Budapest is as Oriental as sandalwood. Even if you did not know that the Hungarians are of Mongolian and Tartar blood, you could spend ten minutes on the streets of Budapest without perceiving it. On every side you see the bright, round, brown eyes of the Orient, set in ever so slightly slanting lids; on every side you hear the sliding, illusive syllables of the language that to western ears sounds like Chinese; every shop front announces the name of its owner backward—Smith John, instead of John Smith—and everywhere are the Eastern motifs in decoration, the subtle, veiled, Eastern curiosity about the stranger, and the charming, half-childish Eastern gaiety that gives the soberest morning the air of a fete-day.

Excursion steamers with flying flags went up and down beneath the spider-web bridges, their decks massed with people as flower-beds are massed with flowers. River boats were stopping at the landings, discharging scores of peasant women whose backs were bent beneath great loads of lilacs. Flowers were everywhere; lilacs waving in the bridles of cab-horses, flowering branches of fruit trees in the hands of sober business men, bouquets in the belts of smartly dressed women. Every second block ended in a tiny park, purple with lilacs, golden with tulips, perfumed with lilies of the valley. Beneath the blossoming locust and chestnut trees that line the business streets, women were selling flowers from great basketfuls, and wagons piled high with blossoms went past on their way to the flower-market at the foot of Elizabeth Bridge.

"And you talk about a subway!" cried Peggy. "Who wants to go under ground when the top of it's like this?"

"I do," said I, inexorable. "I subway; I bathe. Why did we come to Budapest?"

"I don't care why, now we're here!" said Peggy with abandon. "I love it. Mmmmmmm!" The load of lilacs in her arm was to her what catnip is to a cat; in another moment she would have rolled in it. I dragged her down the steps below the absurd little domed kiosk of the subway.

"Good heavens!" said she. "Shades of Childs'!" The subway was tiled in shining white, decorated along the edges with a narrow Oriental pattern in blue and gold. Three or four prosperous-looking, leisurely men, holding large bunches of flowers, stood waiting on the clean little platform. We waited, two–three minutes, five, seven. "The Hungarians are very progressive people," said I. "Think of their sending for Edison and building this subway years before there was one anywhere else!"

"Well, being the oldest subway on earth, maybe it's so old it has rheumatism and can't run any more," said Peggy. Just then one gentle little car slid softly in. It was curved upward on either end and decorated in heavy, scrolly designs; it looked exactly like the little car on the merry-go-round that mother put you into because she was afraid you'd fall off the wooden horse. Its center doors opened, the men on the platform politely stepped back and we entered. The doors closed with a leisurely air; we took the only two empty seats; we gazed out at the men, who still patiently waited, sniffing their flowers. In a moment the little car started, and gently, without clamor or haste, it progressed from station to station; it stopped at each one, but the door did not open unless someone wanted to get off, because otherwise the seats were full, and in another five or ten minutes there would doubtless be another car.

We came up to the sunshine again on the other side of the river, the Buda side. The hills of old Buda rose sharply above us, rugged cliffs down which the pagan tribes of ten centuries ago rolled Saint Gellert, in a spiked barrel, into the Danube. There's a statue of him, triumphant now and haughty in bronze, half way up the (perhaps) same cliff down which he rolled. But if you say "Gellert" in Budapest now, everyone understands that you mean the baths. By saying "Gellert" from time to time to interested strangers, we found our way successfully to the tall building on the river-front, entered the revolving glass doors—and found ourselves in the huge marble-stairwayed rotunda of a hotel. There were palms, deep leather chairs, an unseen orchestra playing softly, and, high above four stories of balconies, a colored glass dome.

For some time we wandered through this enchanted region, until we met a waiter with a tray of cakes. To whom we said, "Bath. *Bain. Baden.* Water. *D'eau. Wasser.* Oh my goodness, *where* is the bath?" He waved us to the stairway.

We mounted, past white marble women and more palms and flowers. We wandered through marble halls with tapestried walls. We passed great expanses of empty, white-linen-covered tea-tables. We came into a hall as large as that of a palace, floored with mosaic, murmurous with fountains, roofed with more colored glass. We looked though enormous glass doors at a tropical garden, where slender jets of hot water rose twenty feet, and clouds of steam floated among jungle plants.

"Is this a bath, or a delirium?" I said to Peggy.

"It's a bath!" cried Peggy, pointing to a shining mahogany door lettered in gold: *"Bains. Mesdames."*

We pushed it timidly open, and were in a large white marble room. On either side hung rows of white curtains, heavily embroidered in every color that makes a rainbow. On the mosaic floor sea-horses were curled into medallions; sea-horses and water-lilies of mosaic were on the high walls, beneath another dome of colored glass where more sea-horses were. This place was inhabited by a woman in a single garment that looked like a pillow-case. She gazed at us, and spoke. We had, of course, no idea what she said. When she saw this, she indicated by gestures that we were to leave at once. Even her fat knees looked reproachful, as she pushed us firmly out.

Again in the hall, amid the fountains, we sought everywhere for explanations, and we found a little desk behind a pillar, where a girl sold tickets. We bought two, in the sign language; the girl took from us eighty kronen, and gave us each a cake of white soap. We returned to the lady in the pillow-case. Smiling, she led us behind an embroidered curtain, gave us two short pillow-cases, and indicated that we were to undress. We closed the curtain and did so. Then we looked up and observed on the balcony above our heads a large and curious crowd of ladies watching us. We hastily put on the pillow-cases.

"Do you feel like an Oriental lady?" I said to Peggy.

"No," said Peggy, "I feel like the dickens."

The attendant put us through a doorway, and left us. We were in a maze of small white rooms, partitioned with glass, floored with marble, and furnished with wicker chairs. Steam radiators filled them with terrific heat. The wicker chairs were too hot to sit upon. We wandered miserably for a time, shifting the melting soap from hand to hand, and then wandered out. The pillow-cased woman paid not the slightest attention to us. At the other end of the curtained room was a large archway. Here another attendant met us and forcibly took from us the cakes of soap. We passed the archway, and stood transfixed.

We were in another enormous room, beneath another stained-glass dome. On either hand was a large pool, indeed a very lake; the bottom of these lakes was Chinese-green tile, and Chinese-green steps led down beneath the water. Sitting on the steps, like figures in a Fragonard painting, were innumerable women and girls, with flowing hair and bare arms and legs like rosy marble in the green water.

They looked at us with interest; we gazed at them with great pleasure. At length we went down the steps, and sat. The water was warm, and lapped our chins. We continued to sit; everyone else did the same. We sat and sat. It was like an enchantment. Nobody moved, nobody spoke, nothing happened.

"How long do we sit here?" said Peggy. I didn't know. One shouldn't take an American impatience into an Oriental bath; on the other hand, I am sure we might be sitting there yet. No one would have minded. At length I rose and climbed the steps. As the warm water receded, a clammy, chilly air enveloped me in the dripping pillow-case. My teeth chattered. I fled to the warm, steam-radiatored rooms we had left.

Instantly the attendant pursued me and chased me out.

"I'm cold!" I pleaded, shivering. "What happens next? Where do we go?" She was not interested; she gazed into space. I fled back into the warmth. She rose and with anger, this time, drove me out again. I retreated to the pool, and sank into the warm water. A hundred eyes regarded me with an attention as calm and unwavering as that of the sea-horses. But Peggy was gone.

I lifted my voice and wailed, "Peg-gy!" The domed glass ceiling echoed. I wailed again. The attendant passed, stolidly. I leaped from the water and besought her with frantic gestures to take me somewhere, to do something. She went on. My teeth were chattering again; the heated rooms were for the moment unguarded. Furtively I slipped into them and stood dripping, hidden by an angle of the wall. Some time passed. Then the attendant entered, pursued by Peggy, who was still clad in the wet pillow-case.

"My goodness," said Peggy, "I'm freezing to death and nobody cares. I told her you were here, but she wouldn't believe it; she wouldn't let me in." We dodged the attendant, in and out among the wicker chairs. "There's a woman who pours soapy water on you," said Peggy, "but it isn't worth the trouble. There isn't anything else but a cold shower bath. It isn't like a Turkish bath at home, not at all. Look out!" But the attendant had got me. She led me sternly out into the cold again, spoke to me violently, and went back for Peggy. She was a thoroughly exasperated woman.

While she was running down the agile Peggy, I found a pile of fresh, dry pillow-cases newly appeared on her table, and joyfully ran to our curtained alcove with several. Dressing, I heard a clamor without, and peering through the curtain I saw the dripping, blue-chilled Peggy standing at bay before a large, strange, violent woman who rent the air with hands and voice. "It's no use," said Peggy. "I haven't got it. My goodness, where would I be carrying money in this measly pillow-case thing? You might just as well keep still," said Peggy, "You aren't going to get it, and that's that!"

"Peggy!" I cried in a whisper. "I've got towels!"

You go to a concert and find, curved behind the boxes, an Arabian-Nights corridor with fantastic fountains. You climb the hills of Buda to the old Gothic church, the Coronation church, and when you enter it—you find yourself in the interior of a mosque. The pure Gothic nave and transept are covered with Oriental designs as rich and intricate as those of any prayer-rug.

And all the tiny incidents of the everyday are as unexpected. You meet a bent peasant woman on the street, and lo! suddenly over her shoulder you see the yellow beaks and placid eyes of half a dozen white geese, comfortably riding to market on a sack of their own feathers. You try to buy a manuscript envelope—and find that Hungarian writers use rice-paper envelopes three inches wide and fifteen inches long, closed at the end like those of the Japanese. In short, nothing that you expect will happen to you in Budapest. That's the charm of it.

It is a charm, I may add, that pursues you when you leave. For no one in Hungary, least of all the railroad officials, knows when or where any train is going. Beyond the new frontiers all is darkness to Hungarians; beyond today all is unknown. "Anyway, why go?" they will say to you. And they cannot understand why you should hasten to catch a train, when probably tomorrow, or next week, there will be another.

That is the reason Peggy did not get her hat. "Send it Saturday, without fail," said she. "We are leaving Monday morning."

"Very well, madame," said the milliner. "We will send it Saturday, or perhaps, if the boy is busy, we can send it Monday."

"But we must leave early Monday morning," said Peggy. "Our trunks must be packed Sunday."

"Are you going back to America?" said the milliner.

"No, to the Balkans," said Peggy. "On Saturday, then, without fail?"

"Why do you not stay in Budapest?" said the milliner. "The Balkans are not interesting, and they are very unhealthy."

"Yes, no doubt. But please be sure to deliver the hat Saturday. Remember, our trunks go to the station Sunday."

"Either Saturday, or Monday, surely, madame. What part of the Balkans?"

"But we leave before breakfast Monday morning," said Peggy.

"Oh, why, madame? There are trains every day," said the milliner.

And on Monday morning, as we steamed out of Budapest on our way—we hoped—to Agram, Peggy sighed. "I suppose," she said, "the hat will be delivered next week, and she will be so surprised because we aren't there. You owe me a hat, Rose Lane; Budapest *is* Oriental."

"Yes," said I. "But if it hadn't been, you wouldn't have got the hat, anyway. And," I went on quickly, before her mind could grapple with that, "we went to get an Oriental bath, and we got it, and you should be satisfied. Aren't you?"

"No," she replied, "I'm not. But, glory, aren't you glad we didn't miss Budapest? Never mind," she said, "we've lived gorgeously for two weeks in the best hotel we've seen yet, and it's cost us both less than forty dollars. The M.F. is rich; the M.F. will buy the hat."

Edelweiss on Chafa Shalit

(*Harper's,* November 1923, 762+)

This story is almost two: the first is a tale of survival in avalanche season over the mountains in Albania; the second is a love story among the tribes there. Written together, the two work to paint a portrait of life among the mountain peoples of Albania. Lane's voice here is exhausted, but joyful, alive, and rich in experiences.

It was not I who found the rare flower. The old gods who rule the Albanian mountains are capricious still, as they were in the days when Zee—whom the Greeks called Zeus—first launched his thunderbolts. "For whom is intended, and who will get, are two persons," the mountain men say. The Chafa Shalit, in rain and sun, had answered my questions with a granite voice that spoke of war and pride and honor. The small flower that blooms there is known to me only from the tale I heard in the Café Frasheri.

The Café Frasheri looks out through white arcades at the sun-drenched street and painted mosque of Tirana. Dusk and coolness are in the low room, where tables stand on sunken flagstones, and the solitary waiter sits smoking a cigarette in a long holder of amber and silver filigree. Time, in his leisurely progress through the dreaming town, stops in the Café Frasheri. Eternity reigns there, with immortal murmur of water in the gutters beyond the arcades and ever-renewed murmur of leaves in the plane trees. There is a mirror on the whitewashed wall, and across its surface pass such shadows as the Lady of Shalott wove into tapestry—shadows of tall men in black-graded white woolen garments and scarlet sashes, moving without sound in moccasins of goat's skin; shadows of tiny donkeys laden with brooms of lavender flowers and pine; shadows of women spinning wool on the twirling spindle; all bright in the hot white street beneath the green plane trees, but cool in the pool of the mirror.

Two of us sat in the Café Frasheri, incongruous figures in peat-scented tweed with blouses and hats from the rue de la Paix, and the coffee grew cold in its miniature cups while Annette Marquis told of her days in the Scutari mountains.

The mountaineers said there had never been such a spring since a hundred hundred years before the Romans came. The waterfalls were frozen, and the rapids of the Lumi Shala boiled black through a crust of ice. There had always been snow on the mountain peaks, but now the world was buried in it. In the village of Thethis men tunneled through snow from house to house, and the children were crying with hunger.

There were five of us, and we were guests; the last sheep was killed for us, and the chiefs smiled, with hands on their hearts, when they passed us the dishes. But there was not enough bread for the village, and our silver kronen were not food. I said we must go. They tried to keep us, but when I insisted, they said that we might get over the frozen snow in the Chafa Shalit and down to the Scutari plain. Four chiefs went with us; you know it is their custom to escort guests to the edge of the tribal lands.

We went in the dark of the morning, with torches to light the way. At ten o'clock the sun came over the eastern mountains, and the white mountains shone and sparkled.

I could hardly go on, for wanting to look at the colors and sparkle. And for weariness, too, for there was no part of me that was not an ache. But the chiefs would not let me stop. So we climbed, till all my muscles screamed with pain, but when I protested, still they urged me upward. Their faces were grim under their turbans, and for the first time I was afraid of them. I did not know why. But I could not let myself be afraid, so I stopped and said that we should stay where we were until I was rested.

"No," the interpreter said, "we will go on without resting. We have come too far to get back and the sun is melting the snow."

I was saying that, nevertheless, I must rest, when he made a gesture so savage that astonishment killed the words. The chiefs were looking upward, listening, and I heard a soft increasing sound like wind in pines. Then the interpreter seized my wrist and said, "Run!" And we ran. Twice the crust of snow crackled and broke under my feet, and I went down into a softness like feathers, down to my armpits. They all pulled me out, somehow, and I saw them shouting while they did it. I could not hear them, for the whole air was rushing past us. When we stopped, the trail we had been climbing was a wide ravine deep cut in the snow, and there was a clean gash through the pine forest below us. The great pines, whose tops had been sparkling above the snow, had been cut off at their roots and carried away. The Albanians knelt where they stood, and crossed themselves, and thanked God.

That was the beginning. If I do not tell you more of what I felt, it is because I cannot; there are no words. I did not know clearly at the time what I was feeling; I know only that I am a different person since that day. We went on, climbing. We could not get back to the trail, but followed along the edge of the gash the avalanche had made. The two peaks of the Chafa were pure and white against the sky above us, and we knew that if we could reach the niche between them we could rest.

But it was not straight climbing up one mountainside. We went over the shoulders of many mountains and across many snow-filled hollows. The sun grew warmer, and all the peaks were shedding their weight of snow. Every few minutes we stopped to listen, and when we heard that sound like wind, we ran. We ran from nine avalanches before I forgot to count them. And the running was dangerous, because beneath the crackling crust there were depths of snow, and in our terror of the avalanches we did not know whether we were above ten feet of it or five hundred. Even the Albanians lost all clear memory of the hidden gorges and cliffs beneath us. Always when we ran I fell through the crust, and always they all stopped until I was pulled out and running again.

We went on, with the soft snow clogging our steps and the crust crackling under our weight. We walked a little distance apart, except that one man was always beside me, and there was no sound except the snapping of the snow crust and a low praying. The chiefs prayed without a pause, asking God to save me. That low murmuring never stopped while we climbed. The hundred miles of white peaks and blue hollows below us were still, with a silence that filled earth and sky more dreadfully than any voice, and the roar of an avalanche drowning the prayers was like a contemptuous condescending—the silence speaking at last to the ears of such midgets as we.

Imagine what it was to us to see on the whiteness before our eyes the blue shadow of another human being. He was waiting for us, and when we stopped in a carefully scattered group he gave us a polite greeting. "Long may you live!" He crossed himself as he said it.

He was perhaps forty years old, and looked as strong as weather-seasoned oak. The thrift and pride of his household spoke in the socks, knitted in a pattern of bright flowers, that lined his new *opangi,* and in the clean beautifully braided white trousers, the combed fringe of the black jacket. The rifle on his back shone with polishing. Friendly laughter and contentment had left their marks around his hazel eyes and on sun-browned cheeks, but the eyes were serious then, and the lips tense.

"I am Gjlosh Marku, a man of the village of Boga in the tribe of Pultit," he told us, when the greeting of the trails was said. "It was telephoned to us across the mountains that the chiefs of Thethis were bringing us a guest, an American *zonya* on her way to Scutari. We replied to him who telephoned, but his voice did not come back to us. So I have come to say to you, all guests are welcome in the village of Boga, and an American *zonya* is thrice welcome. Our village is hers if she honors us by coming. But the Serbs have come down across our lands on the western side of the Chafa Shalit. They hold the road to Scutari, and let no one pass. The Tirana government will not let us fight them. The village of Boga will be happy if the American *zonya* will stay with us as long as she will. But the trails are dangerous today, so I have come to say that if she must go to Scutari, the way through the Chafa Shalit will not take her there."

I thanked him, with my hand on my heart, but what were thanks to give a man who was risking his life to warn me of danger? I felt ungrateful when I said that I could pass the Serbs. He had not understood that the power of my tribe would take me safely where no Dukagjini man could go. We should go on, I said, and was startled by the groan that escaped me when my muscles moved again.

Gjlosh Marku went before us to show us the way, which indeed was marked by his footprints and the flounderings where he had gone down. These we avoided, but again and again I fell. Numbness was coming upon me, and I felt, when the feather softness buried me and I must lie motionless until they dragged me to safety by an arm, that it would be good if they would leave me in peace. Any fiction reader knows that is a desire which must be fought heroically, and I remembered this. But reality is not like fiction, though we try so hard to make it so. I did not go on because of any will of my own, but because the Albanians expected me to do it.

You must realize that we had been climbing and running for twelve hours. The sun was reaching the Chafa Shalit, and the two peaks seemed as far from us as ever. The windy sound of another avalanche came down to us, and again I ran, and again I fell and was dragged out. When I tried to stand I couldn't; I told them to run on and leave me. The interpreter took his revolver out of the holster and cocked it. He said, "I'm sorry, but we must kill you. We can't carry you, and the avalanche might not kill you quickly. If you can't run, we must shoot you and ourselves." His voice was quite gentle and sad. The others slung their rifles off their shoulders, and I heard Gjlosh Marku saying, "my wife." The roar of the avalanche was quite close, and their voices, still praying, were lost in it. You see, I had forgotten their Law of Lec, and that all ten of them must die with me. I got up. But before I could try to run, Gjlosh Marku held my wrist and was pulling me in the other direction. Some obstacle had changed the course of the snow, and when the spray and roar of it had passed, the place where I had fallen was on the edge of the chasm it left.

You don't know how you take for granted the friendliness of the earth, until you see its hostility. At that moment the universe seemed to be playing with us like a cat with a mouse. Even the Albanians were silenced, looking at their old god, the sun, which had betrayed us and now was leaving us. And in a mood of strange mirth I said to the interpreter, "After this, don't mind me. If you're going to do any shooting, please begin with yourselves."

It was enraging to be so weak. Anger took me on for awhile, and then Gjlosh Marku pulled me upward by one wrist. The interpreter walked behind me, saying, "One more step, just one. Good! Now, just one more. Only one step." He said that, urgently, over and over, while the sun sank behind Chafa Shalit and its shadow came down across us. And over and over, through the haze in which I heard that urging and struggled to obey it, I heard another thing—Gjlosh Marku, in his prayer, repeating ". . . my wife . . . my wife."

When we came to the Chafa Shalit the sun shone on us again, and it was like another morning to see the peaks and mounds of shining snow and the glittering forests running down to a glimmer of Lake Scutari, fifty miles away. We fell in the snow, and I seemed to have slept for a long time when the interpreter shook me awake. My Albanians and the chiefs of Thesis were kneeling, with bowed heads, crossing themselves, but Gjlosh Marku was on his feet, telephoning. He swayed and staggered, but he held his thumbs firmly against his ears, and that unearthly call of the mountain people went through the frosty air like the highest note of a violin. He did not rest until an answer came up from the white valley, and then he sat down without firing his rifle.

"Telephoning to his wife," I surmised. We had long ago abandoned all the packs, but a little cornbread had been carried in the sashes, and we sat there eating it.

"Yes," the interpreter said; "he loves his wife."

Wait! I know you will say that this was impossible. I know all you will say: that the Albanians of the mountain tribes are betrothed in their cradles, that husband and wife do not meet until they are married, that their whole idea of marriage is rooted in the idea of the family and the tribe, that they have no faintest conception of love. All your books with their long words tell you that they cannot have that idea. Love is a new thing in the world, a part of western civilization, a pure thing from the cold north brought by the barbarians who killed the worship of Aphrodite and of Venus. Those hidden Albanian tribes, who have held their mountains and their old laws since "a hundred hundred years before the Romans came," can know nothing about love. They have no word in their language for it. All their words for emotions are concerned with war and honor. And wise men say we can have no idea for which we have no words. I know all that. But you see, I met Gjlosh Marku.

It was dark when we came to his house. The night was cold, and the snow once more as hard as ice. From the Chafa Shalit to the edge of the pines it was a smooth gigantic slope, and we did not walk. We lay on the snow at the edge of it, and our bodies went down like sleds—a roar of wind in our ears and a rush of dizzy stars and the heaven of no effort, till terror made us try to stop with a foot dug into the snow. Then a whirling and crackling, and lying still till breath came back and we crawled out on the unbroken surface again. An hour of this falling—little specks of us, shed from the indifferent mountain like raindrops on a window pane, until the sharp tops of the pines came through the snow to meet us, and Mark Gjloshi, the son of Gjlosh Marku, was waiting for us with a torch.

You know the mountain houses, and the line of chiefs drawn up to give you welcome, the shock and flash of rifles firing in the dark, the torchlight on proud hard faces and silver chains, and "Long may you live! Long may you live! Glory to the trails that brought you!" It was good to get into the warm dusk where the fire smoldered on the earthen floor and the goats munched their dried leaves with a tinkling of bells. It was quite a pretentious house. There was a notched log heading up to a little wickerwork room that hung on the stone wall like a bird's nest, and there was a wooden canopy over the fire, velvety with soot, and a hanging basket of ironwork to hold blazing splinters of pitch pine. The floor was neatly swept, and waiting in the ashes of the fire was the coffee pot, like a deep, long-handled spoon, with covered glasses filled with coffee and sugar, and a wooden jar of water, and the little handleless cup.

Of course, you hardly see the women in these houses. After you've greeted them, they fade into the darkness beyond the firelight and are only bright eyes watching you, and a twinkle of marriage belts. I lay down on the warm ground beside the fire without a thought of the wife of Gjlosh Marku, until he said, even before he set the coffee pot in the coals, "Where is my wife?"

His son answered him. He was a handsome boy, about seventeen years old, taller than his father, and blue-eyed. He had hung his rifle on the wall with the others, and was cutting splinters for the lap. All the chiefs were lounging around the fire in that circle you know so well—bodies lean as panthers, in white wool and black wool, colored sashes, and silver-hilted knives, keen eyes and long slender hands rolling cigarettes. It all blurred and went out, and they had to wake me for the ceremony of coffee drinking. Gjlosh Marku needed that cup more than I, and some of my men who were rubbing their feet with snow, but, of course, I must drink first. *"Tu njet jeta! Per te mire!"* The thick hot sweetness of the coffee had roused me when there was a noise at the bolted door, and Gjlosh Marku's wife came in.

She came straight into the firelight, a vigorous woman bringing a scent of pine and snow. She was not beautiful, and had never been pretty. Her face was as browned as leather, but every wrinkle in it was pleasant to see, and her blue eyes were wise and merry. Two neat braids of graying hair hung over her breast to the wide marriage belt; she had gathered up her skirt of black-and-white wool, and under the short petticoat her legs were sturdy in flowered stockings and worn *opangi.* Gjlosh Marku got up at once, and took from the gathered-up skirt a new-born lamb that she had been carrying. *"A ti lodhe?"* he said. "Are you tired?"

Gjlosh Marku does not know any word for love or for home, but I know what there was between those two when they met by that fire, both come alive from the snow and the dark. They simply looked at each other, and she said that she was not tired. Then she went to bring the mother sheep into the house, and Gjlosh Marku went on making coffee.

He helped her later with cooking the supper; there is nothing unusual in that, of course. But there was a difference in their manner of doing it; they worked together not like two workmen, or even like two friends, but as though they were one person. He always knew where she was, without turning his head to look into the darkness, and things were handed from one to the other as from right hand to the left.

"They do love each other," the interpreter said. "I have often heard of them; they are famous in the mountains for this strange thing. And it *is* strange to see. I have not seen anything like it, not only in Albania, but in London or Paris. No doubt, it is common, in America. But to us it is very strange."

Gjlosh Marku himself spoke frankly of it. After we had drunk the coffee and *rakeijia,* after the low table with its chunks of hot cornbread and its central dish of eggs and goat's-milk cheese had been passed from group to group, and we had washed our hands again and lighted the cigarettes of golden tobacco, he proudly directed our attention to her, where she sat in the firelight, embroidering new trousers for him.

"Look now at my wife," he said. "There is no woman like her in the mountains, or even in Scutari. Two thousand kronen she cost me, and I have never spent better money. I would pay for her today four thousand kronen and my goats and my sheep—all that I have. Is she not a beautiful woman?"

We could not truthfully say that she was, but fortunately the question was rhetorical.

"She is as clever as she is beautiful," he assured us. "It is now twenty-four years that I have lived with my woman, and all that I have I owe to her. She knows the ways of sheep and goats, she makes old garments into new ones, she is never idle. She thinks, also. Her counsel is always good."

"It is the good husband who makes the good wife," she remarked, pausing to hold off the embroidery and look at it.

"But how can a man know what he will find when he opens the door to look at his bride?" Gjlosh Marku replied. "She may be ugly, she may be old, she may be of a nature that will make him all his life like a man walking with a hole in his *opangi.* I tell you that I thought many things before I opened that door twenty-four years ago, to look for the first time on the wife who had been brought to my house. But glory to my parents! They had chosen well for me when I was in the cradle. For twenty-four years we have been together in war and in peace, and never have I ceased to bless my parents."

You will understand that I was exhausted, and that in the warmth of the fire it was torturing to keep myself awake, as courtesy required that I do. All the black coffee and cigarettes could barely hold my eyes open, and any part in the conversation was impossible. When next I saw my hosts clearly, the wife of Gjlosh Marku had laid aside her work and was talking steadily, in a low quiet voice, to the interpreter.

"She says that in all the twenty-four years they have had only one sorrow, but it is the heaviest of all sorrows to bear. Durgat Pasha took their oldest son."

Everywhere in the Albanian mountains, of course, one comes upon these traces of Durgat Pasha's passing. The songs of his attempt, with thirty thousand Turkish soldiers, to crush Albania's revolt against the Sultan, the stories of the things he did, and the traces of burnt villages, have made his name to me what it is to the Albanians—something combining with childish terror of darkness with fables of Timurlane.

"But that was eleven years ago."

"Yes. Her son was twelve years old. Durgat Pasha took him to be a soldier in the Turkish army, and whether he was killed or whether he is still a prisoner in Turkey, they do not know. No word has ever come back."

Gjlosh Marku and his wife were looking at each other, not in sorrow, but in consultation. A decision passed between them. She beckoned toward the dark corner where the lamb was sleeping beside its mother, and one of the women stirred and came forward into the firelight. She was not a woman, but a beautiful girl, perhaps fifteen years old. Serious, with downcast lids making black crescents of lashes in the creamy oval of her face, she stood until the woman's hand gave her permission to sit. She wore the white kerchief on her head, the white blouse and white woolen skirt of an unmarried girl; the ends of her braided black hair coiled in her lap, under her folded hands. She was as still as a nesting bird when danger is near, and as acutely intent, through her stillness, on something outside herself. The little sound of a silver chain straightening its links gave my attention the same direction as hers. Mark Gjloshi had moved, with no other sound than that, back from the circle of firelight, and his blue eyes were filled with her.

The interpreter turned to me. "She says, this is the girl to whom her lost son was betrothed. She comes from the tribe of Hoti, and they have sheltered her in this house since her people were killed when the Serbs took Hoti and Gruda. She is a good girl, strong of body and spirit; she is also a good spinner and weaver and a good Catholic. She is of marriageable age, and if it had not been for the wars, she would now be married to the son whom Durgat Pusha took.

"Now if that son were dead, she would of course be married to this other son, since the marriage was arranged between the families. This other boy was five years old, but not betrothed, when Durgat Pasha came, and they have not betrothed him to anyone, because they feared that Durgat Pasha killed his brother. But they have had no news; no one has seen him, living or dead. He may perhaps be in Turkey; he may perhaps come back. They do not dare marry the girl to the boy here, until they are sure that he will not come back. For of course, if he should be alive, he would then have to kill his brother. That is the Law of Lec; that the girl belongs to the man to whom her parents betroth her, and if another man takes her, he must be killed.

"But news may never come. And the girl is of marriageable age, and so is their son. They should be married and have children, but their lives are wasted. They ask you what should they do?"

Gjlosh Marku and his wife waited for my words. The chiefs who lounged by the fire watched me with bright, expectant eyes. Mark Gjloshi was again in the firelight, imperturbably rolling a cigarette in his firm long fingers, and the girl's eyelids fluttered. A more inadequate Solomon never confronted a problem.

"The boy who is gone had never seen her?"

"No; she was with her own tribe then. He was only twelve years old when Durgat Pasha took him, and he would not have seen her until he was fourteen, and married to her. But that does not matter; she was his by the Law of Lec, which must be obeyed. But it is also the Law of Lec that if he dies and leaves a brother who is not betrothed, then she must marry the brother. And it is the Law of Lec that if he is living, and another man marries her, then his honor is blackened until he kills that man."

Desperately I rubbed my eyes, and accepted an offered cigarette. The silence continued while I smoked it.

"Tell them that I am not learned in the Law of Lec," I said. "My tribe has other laws. But as I understand it, when a cause for blood feud rises within a tribe, that is a matter for the chiefs of that tribe to arrange, if possible, so that no blood will be shed. Now it seems to me that if this oldest son comes home after eleven years in Turkey, he will not come for his wife. He has been of marriageable age for nine years, and if his mind were set upon his wife, he could surely have escaped from Turkey during that time. So, if he comes, the chiefs of Pultit should be able to arrange the matter with him. How much was he to pay for his wife?"

"Two thousand kronens."

"Then this son would pay two thousand kronens if he married her?"

"The family would pay that much to her family. But her family is all killed now."

"But she is not killed, so she is the family. Two thousand kronen should be paid to her when she is married."

"Po, po!" Gjlosh Marku agreed. "That much would be spent for her clothes and for the new household."

"Then I would say: If the girl is willing to give up the two thousand kronen, let them be married, and save the two thousand kronen for a few years more. If the brother comes back, let that sum be paid to him to settle the blood feud. And now," I said, "politeness or no politeness, I am going to sleep."

There were some exclamations of astonishment and approval—"Glory to your lips!" the chiefs said to me, hearing my translated wisdom—but I was stretched out on the floor, falling into unconsciousness. Some time between that hour and dawn, half awakened, I felt groping hands and a braid of hair touching my cheek; the girl from the tribe of Hoti was tucking another blanket over me.

That is all. I have told you how I slept all the next day, while my men went back over the Chafa Shalit to find and bring my packs, and how we got to Scutari through the Serbian lines. I do not know what was decided about the marriage in the family of Gjlosh Marku. But you may read all you like in your books that tell how love came into civilized life with the barbarians who destroyed the worship of Aphrodite and Venus. I know how love came into the life of the barbarians, before their language had a word for it.

5.
Mrs. Lane Writes about Herself

In the 1920s, Lane's prolific writing began to pay off. Her short fiction stories were beginning to see print in a diverse number of publications, and her nonfiction pieces were gaining acclaim. Lane returned to the United States in 1924; newspaper clippings from her personal files testify that she was to spend the winter in New York. But her files also reveal that she was striving, with some difficulty, to turn completely away from journalism. She wrote in her diary that journalism was "the most demoralizing form of human activity, made up of catch-phrases, of mere daily opportunities, of shifting feelings." She also took notes on narrative technique, practical rules for narrative writing, and short-story writing. She noted two books in particular: Philosophy of Fiction, *by Grant Overton, and* Aspects of the Novel, *by E. M. Forster.*[1] *Her diaries and correspondence indicate that the shift was due in part to her need to make money to support herself and to help her parents. She wrote Guy Moyston in 1927 about her desire to write only to support her own lifestyle. "I ain't got no art," Lane told him in response to his suggestion that she work at her "art" of writing. "I've got only a kind of craftsman's skill, and make stories as I make biscuits or embroider underwear or wrap up packages."*[2]

1. Diary, July 1925; RWLP, box 21, file 23.
2. RWL to Guy Moyston, July 10, 1927; RWLP, box 10.

The two stories in this section demonstrate the mercenary nature of Lane's literary pursuits as the 1920s drew to a close. Both are written by Lane about herself, and both provide some insight into her character—and her desperation.

I, Rose Wilder Lane, Am the Only Truly HAPPY Person I Know, and I Discovered the Secret of Happiness on the Day I Tried to Kill Myself

(*Cosmopolitan*, June 1926)

Written for Cosmopolitan, *this story shows Lane's intuitive grasp of the marketplace and her need to provide what would sell. Although a storyteller, much of her incentive for writing came from the money it could provide her to live at her leisure. This is a sensational piece that has been used by one biographer to highlight her especially difficult childhood and her difficulty with her parents.*[3] *However, contextualized, it may also be seen as an attempt to sell a sensational story to a public in which she was already becoming well-known.*

I am a happy person even though once I was so desperately miserable that I tried to kill myself.

My present complete happiness is my only claim to distinction, but I realize that it is a stupendous one. It means—almost—that I am unique. If there are other happy persons in this world, they are certainly few. In all the populations between San Francisco and Bagdad I have never met another happy person.

Once upon a time, as we all know, there was a king who sent out messengers to find a happy man and bring back his shirt. After many years they found such a man—but he had no shirt. The moral was that riches don't bring happiness, but that poverty does. The idea is idiotic.

Anyone who may be pursuing a similar quest today is welcome to choose from my dozen or more expensive and very becoming blouses. Any king or millionaire who wishes to abdicate his throne in my favor need only mention it; I accept with pleasure. On the other hand, if I spend my declining days—as I not improbably may—in an old ladies' home, or as a

3. Holtz, *Ghost.*

beggar sitting on the steps of a mosque in Oriental sunshine, I shall not mind. The number of shirts or other possessions that one may have, or not have, has nothing to do with happiness.

Everywhere people want to be happy. Hardly anyone is. Yet there is no reason why everyone shouldn't be happy.

I have learned how to be happy.

The gift of a "happy nature" was not one of those in my cradle. I was not a happy child. Few children are happy. The myth of the happy childhood is created by adults, sighing, "Backward, turn backward, O Time, in your flight! Make me a child again—" The adult is perfectly safe, knowing that Time will not do it.

Children are piteous little creatures confronted by a world with which they are quite unprepared to deal. Pain is their teacher, even in such simple facts as that fire will burn and cats scratch. The best—and the worst—that can be done for a child, is to shelter him from facts; this is merely postponing the natural miseries of childhood to a later date.

In my own case, this postponing was impossible, though my parents did their best. I was an only child; and I was three years old when the last of seven successive years of crop failure on the Dakota prairies ruined my prosperous farmer-father, complications of work, worry and diphtheria left him an invalid, and our house burned. My mother was barely twenty-one. I stood beside her at the window, my eyes just above the sill, on the July harvest day when she watched a hail-storm drive into the ground the hundreds of acres of ripe wheat that would have paid the mortgages.

I was taken away from home, and told nothing—kind adults answering my questions with "Hush!" until I asked no more—during those weeks when my father and mother were expected to die of diphtheria, and I knew it. And later it was I, alone in the kitchen and helpfully trying to put more wood in the stove, who set fire to the house. My mother was still ill in bed. She saved herself and me, but nothing else. I quite well remember watching the house burn, with everything we owned in the world, and knowing that I had done it.

I was always very quiet. No one knew what went on in my mind. Because I loved my parents I would not let them suspect that I was suffering. I concealed from them how much I felt their poverty, their struggles and disappointments. These filled my life, magnified like horrors in a dream. My father and mother were courageous, even gaily so. They did everything possible to make me happy, and I gallantly responded with an effort to persuade them that they were succeeding. But all unsuspected, I lived through a childhood that was a nightmare.

When I was seven, I was a sullen-looking, barefoot child, whose home was a one-roomed log-cabin in the Ozarks. From that log cabin and its few acres of poor, uncleared land my parents have built Rocky Ridge Farm, which would be a country estate in England, a chateau in France. But that year they had only the cabin and their courage. Too poor to buy a cow, we lived on corn bread and a very little fat pork, with wild berries and nuts. I was barefoot under protest. My father and mother would have kept me in shoes, but I pretended that I wanted to go barefoot, and stormed until they let me. I knew what shoes cost.

I have since seen something of human barbarities, in the Near East and elsewhere, but they were no surprise to me. No sensitive child who has gone to school from a poverty-besieged home, in patched clothes, with second-hand books, fails to learn that human beings are barbarous. Schoolmates demonstrate that.

In a few years we were not so poor. My clothes were pretty and my books were new. But the attitude taken toward me by the girls and boys still persisted, and I was too shy, too sensitive, to break it down. I was not invited to parties; I was "left out." I was hurt and lonely. And I knew that I would be happy, if only I could be pretty and popular, "like other girls." It seemed to me that I might escape from myself, be like other girls, if I could escape from the small town.

At seventeen I was proudly self-supporting and in a city. I was not unpopular, I had discovered that I was pretty enough, and my clothes were all that I desired. Living offered pleasant possibilities—and the greatest of these was the escape from living offered by a book. At every opportunity I fled from living and slammed the covers of a book behind me. I did not realize that I was doing this, but when I found Schopenhauer, with his central doctrine that life is pain, I swallowed it whole. It is noteworthy that young people usually do. I was too young to be struck by the fact that Schopenhauer himself spent his life in enthusiastic effort to prove that no effort is worth making.

Then I fell in love. Now people in love are not happy, but they always think they are going to be. Being in love is a delicious process of gathering together all imagined happinesses, and believing that some other human being is the sum of them. You will be happy when you get it. The conclusion is almost mathematical. Millions of young people arrive at it, just as we did. When we were married we would be happy ever after.

The numbers of persons who are not happy, though married, should have suggested to us that there was a flaw somewhere in our reasoning. But it didn't.

We were married, and we were not happy.

In those days a seriously unhappy marriage was supposed to wreck two lives. The point of view is old-fashioned, now when so many lives survive so many marriages. Yet there still exist millions of people who think they would be happy if they were not married. Their thought-process is exactly the opposite of falling in love. They now gather together all their unhappiness, and imagine that wife or husband is the sum of them. They would be happy if they could get rid of it.

The number of persons who are not happy, though unmarried, should suggest that there is a flaw in this reasoning. Marriage, in fact, has no more to do with happiness than material possessions have.

The value of my own experience with marriage was that it made me as unhappy as anyone can possibly be. If only the usual events of the usual marriage had happened to me, I should probably have accepted them and managed to live without being either happy or greatly unhappy. Most people do, and I am not an unusual person. The things that did happen were tragedies, and my unhappiness was no negative thing.

Unhappiness can be as vital an emotion as anger or hate. Mine was. Such unhappiness is not a sentimental woe that expresses itself in sighs. It breeds clear, rational thinking.

Quite simply, there seemed to be no need of struggling through fifty years or so to an inevitable end which might as easily come now.

All this time, to all outward appearance, I had been living normally enough. I decided one morning to kill myself, and at once I felt better. I felt, as one does in illness when the fever goes, a little weak but blessedly cool and convalescent. Some friends had been invited to luncheon; they came, and the little party was quite successful. It was nothing new to me to feel detached and far away, to talk and act through a sense of unreality; I had been doing that for years. After my friends had gone I put the apartment in order, bathed and dressed as usual for dinner. There was a bottle of chloroform in the bathroom. No doubt I had gained my vague ideas of methods of suicide from some forgotten novel. If there had been gas at hand, I might have turned it on. But there wasn't, and chloroform seemed quite satisfactory to me; simple, convenient, and not messy.

No one can be more alive to the ludicrous aspects of that scene than I am now.

I was quite serious. I lay down comfortably on the couch in the living-room, emptied the chloroform onto a handkerchief and buried my face in it. I would not have to live any more, I thought, and felt very peaceful.

Immediately I was aware of a terrific struggle. It seemed to me that every separate cell of my body was vigorously alive, and fighting for life. But I had undertaken to die, and now was determined to do it. I pressed my face against the handkerchief and breathed deeply. To the ultimate instant I drew in the fumes with all my strength, and at the very last thought triumphantly, "My body wants to live, but I am stronger; I have killed it."

I woke with a very bad headache. I thought, amazed, "I am alive." My head ached so badly that it took my whole attention for a time. Then quite suddenly I saw that the whole thing had been absurd. Ridiculous. How could I have been so serious? How could anyone take herself, life, the immense and careless universe, with such desperate seriousness? I felt like a fool. But I was more struck by the fact—never fully realized until then—that I was alive.

I looked about me, and saw strangeness everywhere. It was as though I had never before seen the most commonplace thing. Why, I had not even been fully acquainted with the properties of chloroform, the contents of one bottle in my bathroom cabinet. I didn't, really, know anything about this world. A chair—scores of questions about a chair rushed into my mind, questions whose answers I didn't know. Just to become thoroughly acquainted with the objects in that one room would fill more than one lifetime with interest. Here I was, a stranger in a world filled with things to ask questions about.

It is difficult to put quite clearly the changed attitude that began in me then. It was not a sudden change; some years went by before I fully realized it myself. The old unhappiness would come back, but I was no longer serious about it. I said, "Of course, no one is happy in this world, no one gets anything permanently satisfying, and all of us die. But what does that matter?" Saying "What does it matter?" often enough will kill any unhappiness eventually.

This method, of course, also kills all the bright fancies usually called "illusions," for one has illusions only when something matters a great deal. Illusions are projections of our passionate desire to believe that the world is everything that we want it to be. We believe, for example, that there is good in everyone because we desperately want to believe it. We believe that happiness is just around the corner and that we will have it—"if"—because we desperately want to be happy. When those illusions are smashed now and then by some stubborn fact, we suffer. And we hasten to set up other illusions, usually. But if you don't care whether there is good in everyone or not, if you cease to care even about being happy, then you can begin to find out what the world really is.

It was some time before I realized that I was happy. I had been happy a long time before I recognized that to be happy it is necessary only to be alive, and not to expect happiness from anything else. Human beings lose their way to happiness because they look for it where it is not. So long as one thinks of happiness with an "if," one does not reach it. Happiness is not in possessions, nor in lack of them; it is not in love or friends or travel; it is not in satisfied vanities or realized ambitions. Material things are not particularly satisfying when one has them, and they are most annoying when one does not have them. Love is an experience always desirable, but it is not happiness. Friends are good to have, and very rare. But try to build your happiness on friends, and we shall hear you wailing aloud of sad disappointments and betrayals. Satisfied vanities give a great glow to the spirit, but the vanity will next day be weeping for more of the same. And when we realize our ambitions, we always wonder why we took all that trouble for an end so commonplace.

But, far down under all these varieties of experience, there is a very simple something that is life itself. And if one neither seeks nor expects happiness anywhere else, it is there. Just to be alive, *if nothing else matters to you,* is to be happy.

When death is near enough, most persons will perceive the truth of what I have said. Lay a knife to the throat of the unhappiest wretch, and he will know what I mean. "What! You wish to live? You, with your unfaithful friends, your unhappy home, your pressing creditors?" Indeed you do. With that bright knife-edge against your startled windpipe, nothing else matters. All you want, at that moment, is to live. And you want it desperately. For five minutes after your escape you will be profoundly thankful; you will realize that nothing else matters but the bare life you have been spared.

I cannot advise all unhappy persons to try suicide. Some of them might succeed—which is the last thing they really wish to do. For one sees them every day, in their multitudes, warily escaping automobiles and hastening to doctors to save the lives which they will say are worthless to them. They will say they wish to live because of their hope of that happiness which has, until now, eluded them. But as long as they look for happiness anywhere save in the bare fact of their being alive, it will elude them. And one day, dying, as they must, they will for one brief instant glimpse the happiness of living, the happiness they have had for so many years and have never let themselves enjoy.

Every morning I awake in a most interesting world. I shall die before I have had time to explore even a little bit of it. Every moment that I have is precious to me. Given only one moment in this world, how precious it is! And one never has more than one moment at a time. Having been dead once—though so ludicrously—I found that everything I saw struck upon my mind and senses as something new, strange and infinitely interesting. That sense of freshness, of novelty, has increased and still increases.

It is now fifteen years since I began to enjoy living, and I enjoy it more every day. I have sometimes had a great deal of money, and sometimes none at all; I have had friends, and lost them; I have many times dined at Foyot's, and I have starved on mountains and in deserts; I have been ill and most acutely uncomfortable in caravanserais on the Euphrates; I have been well and comfortable for months surrounded by human beings who were the stupidest, least interesting of humankind; and all the time I have been happy. I am always keenly aware that every experience, of every kind, is a part of living, and I have an appetite for living that grows by what it feeds upon. I'm sorry that I shall die some day, but it doesn't really matter now; for now I am alive. I like being alive. I like it every minute. Just as long as I'm alive, anything that may happen to human beings may happen to me, and I shall still be happy.

How I wrote "Yarbwoman"

(*The Writer,* May 1928)

"Yarbwoman," one of Lane's Ozark stories, was named one of the best short stories in 1927 in Edward O'Brien's "Roll of Honor." Stories included in the roll were believed to be so good as to claim a place in literature, and one scholar suggested that O'Brien's "little magazine" provided a source for identifying talent and an opportunity for fledgling writers to publish.[4] *This piece discusses Lane's contribution to the O'Brien Roll of Honor. The story, set in the Ozarks, is retold in a fictional account of Rose's childhood, and it deals with a deliciously ironic idea, as is revealed in this article.*

The work below is revealing for what it tells us about Lane's work and her writing process, and it reads as a primer for professional writers who need to churn out copy to earn cash on which to live.

As I wrote Mr. O'Brien, "Yarbwoman" is not a story I myself would include in a collection under the adjective he has chosen. It is to me merely a good job of carpentry, not the best even of my own stories. But it does illustrate my method of producing a story which has for its first motive the necessity of paying the rent.

In the middle of the last century the bluffs on Lake Pippin [Pepin] in Wisconsin were infested by rattlesnakes. A man was bitten by one, and died. His brother wore his boots, and also died. The snake's fang was found embedded in the boot. My mother's father, Charles P. Ingalls, was a hunter and trapper on Lake Pippin at that time. He told the story to my father in Dakota Territory in 1870, and my father happened to tell it to me in Missouri in 1923.

Now I have half a hundred notebooks, which I constantly intend to put in order. Each is neatly lettered on the outside, but inside they are orderly as hash. Quotations from my reading, expense accounts, ideas for stories, names that strike my fancy, songs, descriptions of scenery, weather, people, analyses and criticisms of stories and plays, are helter-skelter in all of them. They follow me around the world by parcel post.

4. Alfred Dashell, "What Is Happening to the Short Story?" *English Journal* 24, no. 9 (November 1935): 703+.

One white-hot summer day in Tirana, Albania, I confronted the necessity of selling a story. My immediate future was practically penniless unless I did. Before I sold a story I had to write it, and not one of the ideas simmering in the back of my mind was ready to jell. I tried several on the typewriter, but they would not crystallize. So I began to read the notebooks.

I do not think that this is the correct way in which to write down a story. Nine-tenths of the ideas jotted down in notebooks should die there. They may be perfectly good ideas for someone else to use, but the idea that should make a story will not lie inert in a notebook. It will have some indefinable affinity with the writer, so that it will sink into his mind and slowly take form there, take on a kind of life of its own, and demand to be written. Real stories come out of the subconscious, eventually, and write themselves. Nevertheless, the rent must be paid, and if only a story will pay for it, and no story is ready to write itself; one must be written by main strength and awkwardness.

A page of my notebook said: Pagan renaissance begun in Italy by Leonardo and Guido Brno—England, by Shakespeare and Bacon—reached Germany with Schelling, Goethe, and Hegel. Schiller pantheistic.—*Idea.* Rattlesnake bites man, he dies. Brother wears boots, dies. Snake's tooth embedded in boot.—Ambassador Morgenthau says of Turks that Europe "could not uproot their inborn preconception that there are only two kinds of people in the world—the conquering and the conquered." Is there a people that is neither?

I said, "I'll use that snake idea."

There was a demand for more of my Ozark stories, so I decided to put this story in the Ozarks. But I must invent a reason why a man wore his dead brother's boots. The Ozark hills are muddy only in seasons when snakes are sluggish and don't strike quickly. I must have a swamp. This troubled me, because I know no swamps in the Ozarks, and did not know that the Ozark dialect is used where there are swamps. But I said to myself, "Who will know the difference?" This is indefensible. Had I been in the States I would have verified this point, but in Albania I couldn't; there was not time; I needed the check. As it happens, there are swamps in southeastern Missouri where the people speak the Ozark dialect, so the story was accurate in setting. But that was pure luck.

Having the swamp, I had to provide some motive which would take the characters to it, one after another, so that they would wear the boots. This problem was entirely too much for my staggering mind; I left it to work itself out. I must also provide some false explanation for the successive deaths—some point on which not only the characters, but the readers would fix their attention, so that the boot would not be suspected. If the characters looked at the boot, they wouldn't wear it, there would be no story, and no check. If they suspected an enemy of causing the deaths, they would arrest him for murder, and that brought in too many complications. The deaths must be mysterious. There was nothing for it but the supernatural.

But Ozark folk are not superstitious. They are a shrewd, hard-headed, humorous lot, who would suspect any ghost of being a joker under a sheet. There are no ghosts in the Ozarks, perhaps because even ghosts would dislike being so misunderstood. Stop! Why not a yarbwoman? Far in the backwoods, among people simpler and far more ignorant than any to be found in the Ozarks today, a yarbwoman might be regarded with fearful awe. Especially if there were something unusual about her, in addition to her skill with herbs. Suppose she liked snakes? Solved!

Many sympathetic persons admire and even like snakes. I do. And in California the alfalfa farmers keep black snakes to eat the gophers.

At this point I stopped conscious thinking. I had the story as clearly as I have any story before writing it. I had the kernel of the plot, I had an Ozark yarbwoman, a Florida swamp without its Spanish moss and alligators, the snakes, and two or more unsympathetic characters—they must be unsympathetic, because they were to die of snakebite, and their deaths must be no sorrow to the reader. I stopped thinking, and began to brood, to dream.

Fiction writing is essentially an auto-hypnotic process. No story is real to the reader unless it is real to the writer, and the only experience which we know to be unreal but feel to be real is a dream. The writer is a person whose mind will split in two, so that he can dream and be awake at the same time. The writer's true task is subjective in the very delicate control of this precarious mental process. There is more to be said about this, but not here.

I brooded on this place in the Ozarks until I saw it, felt it, smelled the swamp and the forests. The river, the hills, the roads and trails, the fields, the weather, came quite clearly, and my attention focused itself on the yarbwoman's cabin. I repeat, this is a semi-hypnotic process; all writers use it, more or less, with more or less awareness of what it is.

The focused attention sees everything, every detail, with more keenness of perception than the eye ever has—and with no discrimination whatever. I could have written fifty thousand words about the yarbwoman's cabin. But the part of the objective mind that is still functioning, that is not cut off, selects. It carries on a search for the essential, a discarding of innumerable non-essentials, swiftly done but very gently, deftly, not to disturb the dream. Out of this double process, the subconscious seeing and the conscious selecting, the first sentence—that blessed miracle!—at last comes.

When I was a younger writer, I sometimes wrote and discarded pages of first sentences. Now I seldom put down a first sentence that does not stand. After that, the story "marches." It has a life of its own, like a dream. It *is* a dream—a controlled dream. Harrison rather surprised me by coming into "Yarbwoman." I had not known he was there until he appeared, and had no notion what he would do. He was very useful later, taking me back to the yarbwoman's cabin for the final scene. (Transitions always halt me; they are the hardest points at which to control the dreaming without quite waking up and losing the story entirely.) And as I saw Harrison more clearly and knew him better, I liked him. He was an element that sweetened the story. He added a pathos to it, too, and his being there developed Martha-Rose's character more definitely. If I had thought of him, I wouldn't have put him in. But I didn't; he simply appeared.

My stories are never rewritten; I have done all the rewriting of which I am capable before they are on paper. The first copy would be the final one, if the delicate mental equilibrium could be maintained without wavering. As it is, I sometimes type a word which fails, more lamentably than all my words do, to express the sensation I feel; then I [cross] it out and hang suspended there until a better word replaces it.

The story was written in two days of about fourteen hours each. On the third day a clean copy was typed and hopefully posted. Two weeks later I tore open a cable from Carl Brandt, my agent, and read; "Sorry Yarbwoman refused stop they say too many snakes stop cheer up am trying Harper's."

6.
In Mrs. Lane's Opinion

Lane started her relationship with Woman's Day *magazine almost from its inception, as a flyer for the A&P supermarket chain, in 1937. In her ongoing correspondence with the industrialist Jasper Crane, she wrote that the editor, Eileen Tighe, was as conservative as Lane had become, and was willing to publish whatever Lane wanted to write. At this time, Lane had nearly abandoned her journalism work altogether; her fiction was paying well, and she had turned her attention to politics. The thirties also were consumed by Lane's collaboration with her mother, Laura Ingalls Wilder, on the "Little House" series of children's books, books she referred to in correspondence as "mother's juveniles." Traces of her influence on those books can be viewed by comparing Lane's other work with them, and particularly viewing the work Lane completed for* Woman's Day. *The opinions expressed in some of these works would not have been out of place in Wilder's work.*

A complete archive of Woman's Day *magazine is nearly impossible to find; libraries fail to keep it beyond the current year's issues, and the magazine is not listed in the* Reader's Guide to Periodical Literature. *The only way to obtain these articles in their original form is to comb antique shops or get reprints directly from the* Woman's Day *offices. These articles mark Lane's return from fiction to literary journalism.*

The pieces in this chapter focus on Lane's opinion writing and show her at her most persuasive and political; the editorial columns strongly advocate what we would today call a libertarian political stance. Lane's central thesis was that freedom was the cornerstone of Americanism, and her definition of freedom demanded freedom from government interference in the everyday lives of Americans. The articles here reiterate that theme in varying ways.

Don't Send Your Son to College

(*Woman's Day*, August 1938)

In the 1930s, Lane took in two young boys, brothers who had been left to their own devices during the hardships of the Great Depression. She draws on her experiences as their adoptive mother to lend currency to her opinions here, but her overall point is that people require the experience of working for a goal in order to appreciate the goal itself. This point of view dovetails with her firm opinion that capitalism, and the free marketplace, were the best values for American culture.

We were so poor that I had only one year in High School, and no hope of college. I felt handicapped, and later my life centered in a determination to give my children every advantage I had missed. Last year my older boy graduated from High School and I could have sent him to college. I did not do it.

Why? Precisely because I want him to have every advantage.

I believe there was a time when parents wisely made sacrifices to send sons and daughters to college. Times were harder then, and schooling was difficult to get. Children walked miles to learn to read and write; Lincoln was a hero because he taught himself, without even a slate. High grades were demanded and admired, low grades were a shame hard to bear. From primer to college degree, schooling was a privilege which the student must earn by hard mental work and good behavior. To be expelled from school was the extreme punishment, far worse than whipping.

We all know how completely this has changed. Schooling is no longer an eagerly desired privilege; it is compulsory. If the child does not go to school, the truant officer will compel him. The child knows he must stay in school until he is sixteen years old. He knows that after he has spent the required number of hours in classrooms, he will be given the number of units required by universities. He supposes he will go to university or college, because he would like to be an electrical engineer.

Perhaps I am dumber than most parents. I knew all these facts, and I knew that my boys knew them. Yet for years their school records troubled and baffled me. Semester after semester they brought home passing grades. They were unashamed of a low grade, uninterested in a high one. In vain I tried to spur them to ambition. They listened amiably and agreed to get higher grades next time. "Sure," they said. "It'll be a cinch." Six weeks later they might say, "Gee, I'm sorry. I forgot." Or they might bring home a top grade and listen to my delighted praise. Next time the grade in that subject would be medium or lower. I could not understand it. They had excellent minds. They were fine youngsters, honest, healthy and merry; they were boys to be proud of. And I lay awake nights worried by my failure to awaken in them energy, ambition and earnestness. Nothing they did was well done. In their home tasks there was always an element of the slipshod, of careless irresponsibility, of "Oh well, that's good enough." They never had the deep satisfaction of doing a distasteful job thoroughly, of conquering themselves and their work.

Perhaps they are too young, I thought. Then I remembered boys I knew forty years ago. The thirteen-year-old who sawed, split and hauled wood to pay his school-tuition, and daily trudged four miles and back, doing his farm chores in dark mornings and nights; he is now a great lawyer. I remembered the fourteen-year-old who, when his father died, supported the family and sent younger brothers through school and college. I remembered the algebra, Latin, and German that I studied diligently in spare time when I was working sixteen hours a day, seven days a week, at a telegraph key.

The young today are far happier, healthier, more widely informed about a vastly larger world than we were, but they lack a solidity of character that we had. My boys, too, lacked initiative. Constantly I told them that they must be supporting themselves when they were twenty, and they thought this was reasonable. But in the meantime, whatever they wanted, they did nothing to get it. They had too little money, and accepted that fact; they did not "get out and hustle," as we used to say, and do. When jobs offered, they took them, but they did not see work that needed doing, and thus create jobs for themselves. They did not run under their own power. They always needed a push, a direction, like a good six-year-old. Fruitlessly I tried to prod them into original and vigorous action.

The older boy was a High School junior, athletic, popular, good-looking, intelligent, and wholly occupied in his school's extra-curricular activities, when one day he brought me a grade card showing one solitary high grade. "There you are," he said, and a curiosity which must have been vaguely in his mind for years at least expressed itself. He remarked, "I don't know what you want it for. They'll give me the unit anyway."

Suddenly, in his mildly wondering eyes, I saw the whole extent of my stupidity. All the years of my effort to awaken in him ambition, initiative and effort had made no sense whatever to him, because in fact there was no sense in it.

Words are powerless against fact, and in his life the fact was that there existed no reason why he should arouse his energies. He had to go to school; he could not alter that. He had to stay ten years in school; no effort of his could shorten the time. Being normally bright, he would be given sixteen units when his High School years ended; no effort was required to get them. More than sixteen units were not needed for entrance into a university. Nothing whatever, that he could possibly see, was to be gained by his own exertions or lost by not using them.

Who, in such circumstances, would be active, energetic, ambitious? Which of us parents, if compelled to follow a prescribed routine for ten years, would drive himself unnecessarily to harder work, more self-discipline, initiative, originality, self-reliance? Which of us, during those ten years, would become more enterprising, more energetic, more muscular in mind and character? I know I wouldn't.

But nothing like that will happen to us. We all know that actual living is no inescapable routine. Our lives are a constant struggle to get what we want and keep it. Life itself is a battle. Bare survival in a hostile universe demands alertness, courage, energy, inventiveness and indomitable will. We struggle to survive amid storms, pestilence, drought and earthquake, against the resistance of the vegetable world and the onslaughts of insects, and the rust, mildew and decay of all material necessities. The mere existence of human life on this planet is a triumph of the individual's terrific will to survive.

Every inch of human progress has been made by some man's superhuman effort. Think of the price paid in mind and body for glazed dishes, for the sewing-machine, for machine-woven cloth, for the steam engine, the steam boat, window-glass, the oil lamp and the oil stove, the telegraph, telephone, electric lights. The list is endless today, and infinite in the future, so long as man's energy attacks our environment and changes it.

We must go forward against stupendous obstacles, or slide back. Even in theory not one of us can remain passive and be given food for mind and spirit, except in those societies, doomed to stagnation, where all individuals are like ants or bees, slaves to The State. Our American revolution, which freed individuals from The State, released that energy of individuals which has made us the richest and happiest people on earth.

Here was my boy, a poor boy of the working class. I looked at him—tall, robustly healthy, wearing warm clothes, shirt, collar, necktie, shoes; eating meat, butter, ice-cream, pie, as a matter of course; going to movies and ball-games and the neighboring towns and cities, driving (not without grievance) an aged jalopy; spending nine months a year in school and ready to feel himself a victim of injustice if he did not spend four more years in college. Anywhere else on earth a boy of his social class would be small, puny, undernourished; he would have been sent to work long ago; his clothes would mark him as one of the lower classes, and if he owned fine leather shoes, shirt, collar, necktie, he would jealously preserve them for grand occasions; he would live on bread and cheese, with meat perhaps on a feast day; he would no more dream of owning a car than my boy dreams of a million-dollar yacht, and the idea of going to college would never enter his mind.

What has given my boys such riches? A hundred years ago Americans were no richer than Europeans. Even thirty years ago there was no such wealth in the world as my boy enjoys. All these good things came from the terrific effort each of us made, to escape from privation, to get what we desperately needed and then what we wanted. Would my boy carry on that struggle, so that his children and their children would have more and more good things, as unimaginable to him now as telephones, cars, movies, radios, were to me at his age?

I know now that the best of my life was its hardship. Isn't that true of all of us—the millions of us who for years have been carrying our country through these hard times? Struggling out of poverty developed in us an invaluable strength. Having conquered so much, we know we are stronger than adversity. We do not give way to despair now; we met despair when we were young and we know it for the spur it is. We are not hopeless, for we have been without hope before, yet we lived, we kept on fighting, somehow we beat a way through solid walls and got what we could not hope for but were determined to have. And if we have lost that now, we still have inner strength that we can rely upon.

When I started to school, I was up against the hazards of actual living. To get to school at all, two miles in winter's snows, was a feat in itself. If I did not get there, that was my loss; no one else was concerned except my parents. If I did not thoroughly learn my lessons, that was my disgrace. I studied hard and behaved well, or I was stood in a corner and jeered at by my companions. Before I reached the Fifth Reader, there was iron in my soul, a weapon with which to meet the world later.

My boy had been cheated of that advantage. He had been segregated from hazards, as if in an army or a jail. Nothing had called upon his last reserves of energy. He could not study intensely through a summer and skip a grade, as I did more than once to save time and money; only so many hours in a classroom will get a unit. For ten years, he had been utterly unable to change his environment, whether he liked it or not. He had no experience in actual life, where he must depend upon his own efforts, where bare survival may exhaust his last ounce of determination and creative energy, where success demands fierce resolution, self-discipline, concentration, and where it is man's business to attack his environment and change it.

He said he had to have a university degree, to be an engineer. If I couldn't send him, he couldn't go, and then he couldn't be an engineer. As to what he would do, he had no notion. He said, discouraged, "You can't get a job at anything, nowadays."

Well, would I have done any better, with no more life-experience? It was impossible to get a job when I got one, in the panic of 1907. I got a job because I would have starved if I hadn't; I was hungry when I forced myself into an office and created a life-saving clerk's job at $2.50 for a seven-day week of twelve hours a day, and in spare time I taught myself to telegraph, in spite of the operators hounding me away from the wires. My boy was just as good stuff; the only thing wrong was that he had not had my advantages.

For a whole year I said to him, "If you go to college, you must go." I tried to make him realize that a man must get what he wants by his own efforts. But the fact of his life was that he could do nothing about it. He was as helpless in the school routine as a grain of wheat in the elevator is helpless to change the endless belts. He graduated, and I said, "All right, now go to college, if you can."

It was cruel, but the more atrocious cruelty that we inflict upon our children is in depriving them of hardship, in keeping them helpless in school until they must go into the battle of living without experience of it. I would not give my boy four more years of that weakening protection. If his life is to be any good at all he must be a clean, hard fighter, conquering himself and circumstances. A man must compel his world to give him what he wants. Men always have done this; human beings might have lived as meekly as the animals, but we do not; we change the face of the globe and build our civilizations. Boys like mine, standing up to the Goliath and refusing to be licked, have made the whole human world and created everything valuable that we have.

"I guess I'll have to get a job," he said uncertainly.

"I guess you will," I said.

He left home to look for one, and I let him go. For ninety-seven days and nights I did not hear a word from him. Times were getting harder. He had no special skill, no training, no experience, almost no money. I did not know where he was, and I knew his few dollars must be gone. Winter was coming and still I did not hear from him.

At last a telegram came from a remote town unknown to me. "Am radio expert in largest garage here. Chose this town because it had no radio expert. Company bought me tools and equipment. Doing well and intend to go to university next year. Love."

How he did it I do not know. He was no radio expert when he left me, but I do not doubt that he is a good one now. I learned typing in the same way, on pure bluff and nerve, having got a telegrapher's job that I could not hold without typing and I do not doubt that he will get his university degree. He has an advantage now, more valuable, I think, than any that money could buy; nobody is giving him what he wants, he is getting what he wants. He is running under his own power.

There is all the difference in the world between sending a boy to college and helping a boy who is going to college. I think now that youth today has all the character that we had; let them use it, make them use it, and necessity may make them more unconquerable than we were. At the very least, it will make men of them.

Rose Wilder Lane Says . . . "We Women Are NOT Good Citizens"

(*Woman's Day,* March 1939)

Lane increasingly returned to a theme of citizenship and women's roles in the formation of American politics and ideas. In this piece, she demonstrates one of her trademarks: picking one absolute point of view and sticking to it. Her thesis here is that women have not exercised their rights as citizens and fail to participate in civic life to the degree that they should. In fact, Lane addresses a broad public that has failed to take responsibility for its government, and again draws on her experiences as a mother—and grandmother—to make her points. The italics within the article are her own.

For years I have felt capable. People ask in wonder how anybody can know as much as I do. I know very little, of course, but I did think that I knew enough for practical living.

Luckily I was born poor, and soon knew the long hungry depression that we called "The panic of '93." So I can find something to eat in any field or forest. (This came in useful when I and my pack train were lost two days without food in the Dinaric Alps.) Give me seed and earth and weather permitting, I can harvest, thresh, stack, or dry and string and store them safely, too. Give me a pint of hard field corn, some wood ashes and water, and I will keep you from starving for one day more.

After two years we got a pig and a cow. From a cow I can make firm butter and sound yellow cheese. I can turn every bit of a butchered hog into good food. If you are so rich that you need not eat the pork rinds, I can make soap.

I darn, patch and mend anything from clothes, shoes, tinware to farm-tools and typewriter. I am a good carpenter, painter, wallpaper hanger, amateur electrician. I can handle any domestic construction job.

I am a telegrapher and a typist, file-clerk, salesman, executive. I knit, embroider, crochet, design and make patchwork, appliqué, hooked rugs and so on; I weave and spin; when hats were expensive I made mine. I am an expert dressmaker and, if I do say so myself, a swell cook.

I have lived in almost all our States, and nearly all countries of Europe and Asia Minor. I know three languages, and get along in three more. From a lucky lack of schooling, I cram every spare minute of learning. My library is now source-material, and years ago I discarded college textbooks because they were full of errors.

All this time I have earned my living, supported one to ten dependents, and since 1916 paid an income tax.

I do not mention all this to bother you with my minor worries, but only to show that I thought I was handling my own affairs, not badly.

No one can say that she brings up a child. The mystery of God's creation is in that growing up. I doubt that my anxious meddling with it did much good; the best thing I did for my youngsters was to love them (I couldn't help that) and let them grow. Anyway, all three turned out splendidly, and I have a little granddaughter who—now don't think I'm prejudiced; it isn't because I'm her grandmother; you'll see for yourself that she is the most remarkable child.

So, I did feel like a capable woman. Given what I had to do with, I thought I had done pretty well.

I bought a little house set in old orchard trees and grapes and shrubs and flowers. Just the kind of little house I like. I lined a good deal of it with bookshelves and moved in my books. Now I had a place for really studying.

When all this is yours, and you made it yourself, and you are conscious of no great failure or lamentation in the years of your life that are gone, then self-satisfaction rises up in you. And I suppose it does need taking down.

I discover that I have never done the one thing most important. The one thing I imperatively should know, I don't know.

As an American citizen I am a complete washout.

All my live I have earned, or more than earned, everything I ever got. Or so I thought. I do not like anyone who gets something for nothing—the woman who always comes to parties but never gives one, the neighbor who borrows and does not return, the man who doesn't see a restaurant check until someone else is paying it. I despise them.

Yet I could do what I did and get what I have, only in America, only because I am an American citizen. All my life I have used the greatest advantages that human beings ever had in all history, freedom and opportunity and securities and protections that exist nowhere else, that men and women have lived and died to create and keep and give to me, and I have never done one thing to earn my right to them. I have done nothing whatever to protect that right for my children.

And when I realized this, and asked myself what I could have done, or can do now, I did not know.

Oh, I know the principles. I know the history. I know political philosophy since Greece. I even know American political philosophy, though in all our schools and colleges there exists not one textbook to tell our children what America means; not one.

I know what is actually happening now, in Europe and Asia and here. I know facts; such facts as this: In every country on earth during the past two hundred years, the actual and the legal right of common people to control their own lives has depended on the share of their earnings that government does not take from them in taxes. Every increase in taxation is a threat to our children's liberty.

But what do I do? I did not know.

I have been living my own life, hindered by nothing but circumstances and the limits of my own abilities. Everywhere else on earth, people like me are controlled and kept in their place and class. My freedom comes from the fact that this is a government of the people by the people. I am one of the people. But in all my life I have never done any governing.

Of course I have voted. But the miserable subjects of Russia and Germany vote, and so did the people in ancient Rome who were fed and amused or burned alive at the Emperor's whim. Voting is not governing; it is giving someone else the power to govern.

I do not even know the men I vote for. They tax me; I must pay. By far the largest share of my taxes is collected and spent in my own community. Who is spending that money? What is he spending it for? Is he as thrifty as I am, does he get lowest prices for best quality, is he pinching my pennies and trying to reduce taxes? I do not know. I've never even met him.

It is appalling. It does not seem possible. The whole value of my life comes from my freedom. Every day in Europe now, hundreds of men and women are killing themselves rather than submit to tyranny. Americans fought two desperate wars for freedom, such a little while ago that our grandfathers knew men wounded in those wars. Living men remember now the days when Lincoln was praying that government of the people by the people should not perish from the earth. From the earth, because such government only exists in America.

And already I have so forgotten what my right to govern is worth, and what its loss would mean, that I have not even bothered to use it. I did not know how to use it.

I cannot run my house by giving it a lick and a promise every two years. I cannot govern a child by paying a nurse to keep him out of my sight. I cannot govern my country by electing strangers to office and calling them "The Government," as if they were some force of nature like the weather, which I cannot control and for which, therefore, I am not responsible.

I am responsible for government. To make us free, the founders of our Republic gave you and me the right to govern it. A right is a responsibility. Whoever has the right to govern a child, is responsible for the child.

But no one can be responsible for governing, without the power to govern. I cannot long keep my right and my power to govern myself, and get out of the responsibility. Someone must be responsible, and he must have the power. If I keep on letting strangers govern me, some day they will have to take the power to make me obey them. Then my children will be subject again to the old tyranny that Americans drove from this continent.

That is a plain fact. I am trying to think what to do about it.

I have remembered a Nebraska farmer whose taxes were too high. He wondered if the men he elected were spending the public money as carefully as he spent his. He found a neighbor who wondered, too. They chipped in a few dollars apiece to hire an accountant to go over the books. Any citizen has a right to examine the public accounts.

The farmer found that the politicians were carelessly buying supplies at prices higher than those he could get. He took the figures to the newspapers; editors of the party out of the office will always print such news. In his spare time, the farmer kept on doing this year after year, while angry voters kept throwing either party out of office, and politicians worked as they never had worked before to reduce spending. Tax rates came down.

Taxes are still kept down, in Nebraska. And when Nebraska built the most beautiful modern capital on earth, the State treasury paid cash for it; ten million dollars. Cash; no borrowing, no bonds, no financiers' profits, no debt for Nebraskans to pay with interest.

That is governing. Any citizen can do it. One woman, by herself, can do that in her community. It will not cost much money nor take much time. All it needs is the doing. That is one thing I can do.

I could not hire someone to do my housework, and pay no attention to it. Why should I expect a politician to work hard, be honest, dig out dirty corners and kill cockroaches and slave to save my money, when he knows that I do not ask nor care what he does?

I hope to learn more about being an American. But this is something to begin with. I am going to meet and know my servants in public office; I am going to know exactly how they spend my money. And when their work pleases me or doesn't please me, I am going to tell them. I begin right now. You and I can be just as good Americans as the Nebraska farmer.

Don't Tell *Me* How to Live My Life

(*Woman's Day*, September 1939)

As a self-educated woman, Lane was impatient with academic "experts" who, in her opinion, seemed to dismiss common sense or else dressed it up by verifying its validity through some sort of study. A thread that runs through some of her opinion writing is the necessity of people taking their educations into their own hands, and the validity of such self-education. In this article, Lane urges her readers to recall common sense and to not follow blindly the "expert" opinion.

In days not long ago, which you are too young to remember, women were downtrodden. Their place was in the home. They didn't have wages, they didn't have votes, they hardly ever had a divorce. But they were expected to have characters and minds of their own. And they did have them; they had to.

I remember when they had. And if you have never spent a rainy afternoon with files of *Godey's Lady's Book* a hundred years old, you have no idea how they restore your self-esteem as a woman. From every page you breathe the unquestioned assumption that the ladies in those quaint clothes were entirely able to manage their own lives and that, with God's guidance, they were doing so competently.

Today you can't pick up a new magazine or go into a bookshop without being told in print how to be popular, how to make friends, how to live alone or get a husband, how to hang onto him when you've got him, how to get along with his mother, how to bring up the children (and precisely what kind of children you must make them be), how to make home happy, how to make a guest feel welcome in your house, or how to be a welcome guest, how to treat an adopted child, how to keep your friends. Never before was every woman so thoroughly told how to live.

It's fantastic. What makes all these writers assume that an ordinary, normal woman is unable to live her own life? Why do they believe that all the answers to all the problems of love, marriage, motherhood, friendship, happiness, are in the back of the psychology book?

People used to think that it is our business to work out these problems for ourselves with the help of faith and prayer. Neither Freud nor Dorothy Dix told Priscilla Molines how to marry John Alden, when he wouldn't ask her. Nobody told Mrs. Washington, a widowed "poor relation," how to guide her son's attitude toward his more fortunate cousins so that George would not feel inferior.

You'd think that Mrs. Houston knew how to raise boys; all her sons turned out well except Sam, who developed low tastes and wasted his youth in idleness with lazy Indians. The city in Texas is named for Sam, not for his good brothers.

Mrs. Carson's Kit did not finish his soundly chosen vocational training as saddle-maker; abruptly he disgraced the family by being a runaway apprentice. So later Kit Carson guided Kearney to California and Kearney added the West to the United States.

Mrs. Rebecca Hoover never heard of child-psychology or hygiene or dietetics, but while running a farm and a community and being a force in Iowa's politics she bore nine children and adopted nineteen more, and raised all twenty-eight to live healthy long lives as widely respected men and women.

Now don't misunderstand me. Nobody is more enthusiastic than I am about the widespread knowledge and material abundance that make

Americans today the healthiest, tallest, most energetic people on earth. Just try to turn the clock back forty years, to the days when tomatoes eaten with sugar and cream were an August dessert, when an orange was a Christmas treat and grapefruit had never been heard of; when fresh vegetables, fresh fruit, fresh eggs and good milk were obtainable only on farms and only in the summertime, and winter was supposed to "thicken the blood" so that before spring it must be thinned with doses of sulphur and molasses; try to revive those days when Saturday night meant the weekly bath and warm weather in June was the time for the cautious yearly shampoo—just try, and you'll hear from me a sky-piercing howl.

I am all for the great complex of science and business and industry that grows in American freedom and constantly distributes them more widely. You hear me cheering for the American standard of living that has been climbing for a hundred years and is still going right on up.

But when we say "standard of living," we are speaking of material things and the health and pleasures that come from material things. Science deals with material things and produces material good. How can we say that psychology, the study of our human selves, is a "science?" Human beings are living souls. Science is knowing, and life is unknowable. Life is a mystery.

Two plus two are four, and H_2O is water, every time. But Mother plus Susie at breakfast is not the same thing as Mother plus Susie at bedtime, as everyone knows. The relationships between parents and children, husbands and wives, friends, lovers, neighbors, are infinitely various and variable, and in them the future is unknown.

None of us is wholly like another, none of us ever repeats experience. Today we are not what we were yesterday, tomorrow we will not be precisely what we are today. So how can one human being tell another how to live?

For good or bad, for better or worse, each must live his own life. No one else can. No one else ever knows what, actually, to us, our life is. To live as best we can is an individual responsibility.

We all know this is true. But there is something overwhelming in the masses of instruction and advice that we are getting from all sides.

Listen, for instance, to the bland child-psychologists. Maybe I am weaker-minded than most, but there was a time when I knew so much child-psychology that the mere sight of a child gave me the jitters. I couldn't be my natural self (with the normal effort toward such improvement in me as I might be able to make). I couldn't meet a child simply as a young human being himself. My head was full of rules and the rest of me was rigid with terrible responsibility.

The rules, and the awful warnings, were something like this: Never injure the child's individuality. Don't keep him from smashing the furniture, or he'll have an inferiority complex. Remember that one thoughtless word now may ruin his whole life. Whatever he does, control yourself; NEVER SHOW ANGER. Never punish; punishment is a brutal use of superior strength. Always explain fully, always reason with the child, sweetly and calmly. Remember that a child has no reason and no memory, therefore keep right on repeating your reasoning with him, always calmly, always sweetly.

Well, all that is old-fashioned now, but it was the gospel of child-psychologists then. Now they have another gospel, for fashions in psychology change as swiftly as fashions in hats. And I think they're all nonsense.

I think this whole mass of instructions for living is pernicious nonsense, because it diverts our attention from our real business in living, which is simply to try to become better human beings.

True, we don't know enough to live as well as we want to. Probably there isn't a woman living who doesn't cringe in remembering the mistakes she has made, nor one who doesn't wish she could be sure what is best to do now. But no one else can know our problems even as well as we know them; and if we may not understand them, how can anyone else? Taking one's troubles to the psychologist, or discussing them with a friend, is a flimsy substitute for taking them to the Lord in prayer.

In whatever words you may state the fact—and there are many ways—the fact is that the only wisdom, the only strength, that we can use must be within ourselves. And whatever name we give to the source of wisdom and strength, we know that the name is the name of a Mystery that no man claims to comprehend. It has not been revealed by telescopes nor captured in the depths of "the sub-conscious."

We grow confused in the chatter of too many words, too many glib and shallow thoughts, too much advice. We grow so confused by the external world that some of us say we do not believe in God. And those words are meaningless, for we know that we live, and that life is a mysterious yearning for a greater goodness that we have. To say that we live is to say that we believe in the existence of a Goodness to which all men, in all languages, have given a name that, in English, is God.

Let us stop listening to the advisers who so arrogantly and complacently tell us what to do with the problems of our lives. Must we tell an adopted child that he is adopted? How can we hold our daughter's confidence? Our husband's love? How shall we keep the family together in the evenings? Or shall we? What will make our homes attractive to our children's friends? Should a mother-in-law live with us? How can we teach our children to tell the truth? The answers can come only from ourselves, from the wisdom and truth of our hearts.

Every act that does not spring from the truth of our own selves is false to ourselves, and what good can come from falsehood? Our lives express what we are; our pretenses, however well-meant, do not deceive, because they express a falseness within ourselves. Certainly, we should never let our angry passions rise. Our job is to be sincerely more loving than angry. If for an instant we are more angry than loving, I say that an honest outcry or even a slap is better for any child than a mother's hypocrisy. Let us cherish our human desire to be our best selves and to become better, but let's honestly be ourselves, living our own lives by the light that is ours and trusting in God.

We Who Have Sons—
Will They Be Killers in Uniform?

(*Woman's Day,* December 1939)

Lane wrote this piece at the end of 1939, disturbed at the news of the war in Europe. Her travels throughout Europe had given her a deep love for its people, particularly those of Albania, and she well remembered the devastation she found there just after the First World War. Lane's experiences writing about what she had seen in the aftermath of the first war probably influenced her opinions about the looming second war. Throughout this work, strength of purpose underscores her lament: "What can it profit us to gain the whole world and lose our own soul?"

While the candles burn on my family's Christmas tree this year, I want to remember only that life is good.

Centuries upon centuries after Abraham was dust in the cave of Machpelah, Christ came to tell mankind of the fatherhood of God, and to say, "One commandment I give unto you, that ye love one another."

Now, nearly two thousand years after the Star shone over Bethlehem, we celebrate the birth of Christ. In America, in 1939, we light the mysterious fire on the evergreen tree, for our children.

Let us be honest: this is not a merry Christmas. Only very little children can be merry now. Christians are killing Christians in half of Christendom, and we will hear the guns through any chime of Christmas bells.

But for a little while I want to realize that the wrongs and miseries of this world are only temporary and that our human growth toward a better life on earth is eternal.

Measured against the long upward struggle, it is only yesterday that twelve men first heard the commandment, "that we love one another." We have only begun to ask of God, "Thy will be done on earth as it is in Heaven."

Our hope of a world in which men will be kind to one another is a new hope, not even known to many peoples on this dark and bloody earth. The peace of the world is a new goal, which human beings are only beginning to see and to try to reach.

I want this Christmas to strengthen my faith in the goodness of life, and in the power of that goodness to overcome evil on earth and within myself. Something of that faith is shining around all the Christmas trees on earth, the little trees in Germany and England and all the trees that light the very continent of our America.

Too soon the lights will go out on our Christmas trees and before the new year begins we will be asking again, "What should America do? How can Americans act for good, in this immediate world, in this horrible convulsion of history?"

All the terrific power of hate and greed and horror will press upon us and there will be confusion in our minds and anger in our hearts. The cruelty in the world will breed hate in us, and ruthlessness will breed an unreasoning fear, and a clamor of voices will whip up hysteria, until like horses rescued from a burning stable we may insanely try to end our fears by rushing back into the roaring fury of torture and death.

Now while we are quiet, let us summon all we have of faith and strength and calmness, to keep us quiet and strong through the coming days.

President Roosevelt has given us a solemn pledge: "This nation will remain a neutral nation."

If ever a people stood firm and united behind its highest representative, I think that the American people should stand now like a wall of rock supporting our President in that pledge.

Even in the words he spoke after he gave that solemn promise, there was a hint of wavering strength. More than any of us, he is suffering the terrific pressures that try to make him break that promise. Not since Lincoln has any President more needed a people determined to help him keep America safe for the world.

I honestly think I can put aside my personal emotions in this matter. Like all American women, I know that my life is at stake. I have two sons old enough to be conscripted.

I did not bring them up to be pacifists. I am not a pacifist. I have found that every hour of every day is a battle of one kind or another, and I do not believe in enduring wrong nor in letting evils increase. I believe in fighting injustice, dishonesty, hypocrisy, cruelty, wherever they appear. I want my boys to be fighters. I brought them up to be Americans, educated in freedom and responsibility.

If America goes again to war in Europe, their freedom vanishes. But their responsibility will remain. They must decide for themselves whether they will go to Europe as killers in uniform or whether they will endure the greater suffering of refusing to go. Whatever they do, I trust they will do for a principle that is worth to them the sacrifice of their lives.

For if we permit the President's pledge to be broken, their lives will be sacrificed, and mine, with the lives of all American sons and mothers.

But there are causes worth dying for, even worth killing for. This question, "What shall America do?" is larger than any question of our personal emotions, or of our lives. Upon our answer to this question depends the future of our country and of the world.

Like everyone else, I can answer it in the ways called "practical." There are two "practical" answers, and one is that war makes profits. Everyone makes money in war time. No one is unemployed. Wages soar, farm prices sky-rocket, every little shop and business booms. Every man and woman who stays at home can become drunkenly rich, as we all did, twenty-four years ago. This is the truth; let us face it. Will you, will I, give up the job, the raise, the prosperity within our reach, to keep peace on the three thousand miles of earth that is American?

The other "practical" answer is the question: "What did we get out of the last war?"

I lived through the war; I was nearly 30 years old when the Serbs killed Austria's Crown Prince in Sarajevo. And during the decade after that war I knew Europe from London to Sarajevo, from Berlin to Cairo.

Americans were neutral when that war began. Our President promised us neutrality then. But we did not then know, as some of us know today, the power of the forces, outside us and within us, that we must withstand.

England seemed nearer us because our language grows from English, but we had not forgotten that England is our ancient enemy. We remembered that in our moments of weakness England tried to break our country apart, that France seized our threat of war and forced England out of Venezuela. We had seen England seize South Africa from peaceful Dutch farmers, and herd them into unspeakable concentration camps. We saw England holding India, Egypt, and much of Africa in crushed subjection. We knew that England is a kingdom, ruled by hereditary aristocrats, and ruling an empire of subject peoples exploited for English profits.

We had had only one slight encounter with Germany in the Philippines. A younger country than ours, Germany was picking up the crumbs of Asia and Africa that England and France had not devoured. We owed our northwestern frontier to the German Kaiser, who arbitrated our threatened war with England over that territory. We knew that Germany was an absolute monarchy ruled by the Kaiser, and ruling an empire of subject peoples exploited for German profits.

Americans saw that war as one more war between European empires that had been at war for centuries. In America we had begun to build a new world on a new principle, the principle of human rights. We hoped that principle would some day prevail in Europe, and bring those little countries the peace that it has spread across our great continent. But with the endless repetition of wars in Europe, we thought we had nothing to do.

For two years we watched that war. Then we re-elected President Wilson because he was keeping us out of it. We re-elected him in November; in April we were in the war. The President called for volunteers. In two months, only 80,000 men volunteered. It was plain that Americans would not willingly fight in Europe. So our men were conscripted. Four million were conscripted; two million were shipped overseas.

Meanwhile we all surrendered ourselves to a war-frenzy. Americans actually believed, sincerely, that war would end war, that we were fighting for democracy, that with slaughter we would reform the world. We believed that all the world's evil was in the Kaiser, and we screamed, "Kill the Kaiser!" We fought to end dictatorship, and our men went to do it, singing, "We won't come back till it's over, over there!"

In America, we had dictatorship. Dictatorship is believed to be necessary in modern war. Therefore, in America, our American rights of free speech, free assembly, free press, were suppressed. Men were sentenced to twenty-five years in jail for saying that war is evil. Police power enormously expanded and often fell into the hands of stupid and brutal men. We who remember the barbarities of those days would rather forget them. But we remember that when mob-hates are loose and police power rules, when an unpopular opinion is a crime and American rights do not protect us, there is no escape from barbarities.

For two years, four million men were taken from productive work; every American life was shattered; all our energies poured into hate and destruction.

We won the war for England and France. We dethroned the Kaiser; we forced the German people to accept the form of government we decreed. We remade the map of the world; we created the League of Nations. Then we came home leaving Europe in the hands of England and France.

For ourselves, we got a boom and a collapse, the drunken Jazz Age, the insanity of speculation that always follows war, then its inevitable crash, and our present depression. Today, where is the German Republic? Where is the League of Nations? Where are the huge war-profits that every American worker and every American farmer made during the war?

These are the facts of our recent experience. Upon them, we can base our "practical" conclusions.

But I do not believe that "practical" considerations are really practical. Man does not live by bread alone. What can it profit us to gain the whole world and lose our own soul? I truly believe that it is more practical to preserve the spirit than the body. Every living body dies. It is the spiritual value of our lives that is indestructible.

This is not a matter of faith alone; it is a simple fact of history. The treasure that is ours to guard in America is not our marvelous material wealth that is constantly decaying and being renewed, nor our lives that will soon end and be forgotten; it is our ancient inheritance of spiritual values, the meaning of personal freedom that comes to us from Abraham.

Abraham declared that God is the Spirit ruling heaven and earth, and that man is a soul, free to choose good or evil, and responsible to God for his acts. No one can be responsible for the good or evil of his life, unless he is free to control his life.

Abraham's descendants could not endure the burden of such responsibility; again and again they begged for a king to rule them. Moses told them to obey God's commandments. Gideon refused to be their king, saying, "Not I nor my sons shall rule over you, but God shall rule over you."

They were too weak to keep freedom in the world; Babylon carried them back to captivity, Rome conquered them.

Christ attacked even the authority of their priests, and scorned the power of Rome. His every word assumed the freedom and responsibility of each individual, and a Roman governor sentenced him to death as a rebel against Roman government.

Empires vanish. Chaldea, Assyria, Babylon, Persia, conquered their world by force of arms and ruled it and are gone. Egypt is gone, Rome is gone. But in a world where no man had freedom, for thousands of years Abraham's belief in freedom survived, until—barely a century and a half ago—a few men in Philadelphia staked their lives upon it. They said to the world: "We hold these truths to be self-evident, that all men are created equal and endowed by their Creator with certain inalienable rights, that among these rights are life, liberty—"

The word was a bombshell. The idea of liberty attacked the Divine Right of kings that was the foundation of civilization, a hundred and fifty years ago. Frenchmen, Germans, Italians, were serfs bound to the soil; every worker was subject to his guild. Englishmen, the freest men on earth, were subject to their King even in religion. Trade, commerce, farming, manufacturing, shipping, clothes, manners, were controlled by rulers. It was the King's business to say what cloth the housewives might weave on their looms, what trees a farmer might cut on his land, how many threads of warp and woof the weavers must put into cloth, at what prices the merchant might buy and sell, and where the ships might sail. At the King's order, his subjects were seized for army and navy, or sold like cattle to serve in another King's armies. At the King's pleasure his subjects were arrested, imprisoned, tortured, executed or released.

Suddenly into that ordered world a word came from America: Liberty. And farmers in Massachusetts, leather-clad frontiersmen in Virginia, took muskets in their hands to fight a world-empire, for freedom. They fought to cut America away from Europe, so that they might establish here the first nation founded on the principle of human freedom.

That was yesterday. My grandfathers' fathers fought in that war.

Here in America, men established religious liberty, our right to worship God in our own way and obey our own consciences. They secured free speech, free assembly, free press, universal and classless education. Here they set up a Civil Law, superior to any human ruler. Here they established impersonal justice—our right, if accused of crime, to know the charge against us, to defend ourselves in public, to jury trial, to appeal from an unjust verdict. Here every human being was made safe from arrest, from search or seizure of our persons or our property, without due process of law.

All these rights are new. They are not two centuries old. Over most of the earth they have never yet been known at all. We are shocked today because Germans and Russians do not have them. No one dreamed of having them when my great-grandfather was born.

For forty years, the world expected the American Revolution to collapse at any moment. Russia did not recognize our new government for half a century. But this experiment's incredible survival, its even more incredible success, was affecting western Europe. The English greatly modified their old government. Frenchmen, Italians, Germans attempted similar revolutions that never entirely succeeded and now have wholly failed. And from all that old world its oppressed peoples rushed to America, to this revolutionary experiment, a thing untried in all history—a nation founded on the freedom and the human rights of man.

We Americans are of all nations, all races, all kinds of humanity. In five generations, we have not made anything like heaven on earth. But we have become the kindest, the most idealistic, most generous, most nearly classless, most generally well-fed and comfortable and healthy, by far the least unfortunate, the least hungry, of all the peoples in this real world. And we have brought enduring peace to one continent on this earth, a continent many times larger than Europe and inhabited by all European peoples.

God knows that free men are full of faults and sins, and not all that we do is good. But everything good that we have accomplished, we have done because we are more nearly free than human beings have ever been. And every wrong in our country comes from the failure of individuals to understand that no one can be free without moral responsibility.

We must give America time. We must save for our children this chance, this time in history, another fifty years, another century, in which to understand the responsibilities of freedom and to make America more nearly what it was meant to be. Let us not be overwhelmed and carried back to captivity, as the children of Israel were.

What we see today in Europe is not new; it is the old tyranny, recovering from the shock of American liberty. Hitler, Stalin, Mussolini are absolute monarchs; so were the monarchs from Nebuchadnezzar to Napoleon. There is no new danger to us in Europe; the same danger was even more threatening and nearer a hundred years ago when America was young and weak. European dictators were in America then—when Spain ruled Florida and Texas and California, when English troops held Michigan and Ohio, when France owned half of the Mississippi valley and Russia had Alaska. On the whole earth then, human freedom and human rights existed only in the little new republic on our Atlantic coast.

On the whole earth at this moment, human freedom and human rights exist only in one great power, America. War has extinguished them in England's limited monarchy and in France's bureaucratic republic. War will extinguish them here.

I think that our American heritage of liberty is the most precious thing on earth today, the most valuable thing that we can save for the future of the world. Here on our American soil, we hold freedom and peace and good will to men. I think it is the duty of each of us to cherish them, to protect them by every act of our lives. I think we must be vigilant now to preserve them in a world overwhelmed by the forces of hate and destruction.

I will not willingly surrender again the peace of America, the lives of Americans, the American rights of free speech, free assembly, free press, protection from lawless search and seizure—I will not willingly surrender these precious things once more to war's dictatorship.

Every person to whom I can speak will hear me say this, and will hear me say that we must stoutly uphold our President in his pledge: "This nation will remain a neutral nation."

And this is my New Year's resolution: Week by week, until Europe makes peace in Europe, my representatives in Washington shall hear from me, and from every person whom I can remind to spend a penny for a postcard. No pressure can make our President black-out peace in America, so long as the voice of the American people—your voice and mine—continues to repeat in Washington, "This nation will remain a neutral nation."

Never before has every woman been so responsible for great and immortal values. For here in America our heritage of liberty has given each woman the rights of a human being and has made her responsible for saving these rights, for herself and her children. An American woman has power, the power of a citizen's vote. Our representatives in Washington know that a citizen who writes to them is a citizen who knows her power and will use it.

If we do not use our right to self-government, we cannot expect to keep it. All dictators from Nebuchadnezzar to Hitler have sincerely believed that ordinary people have not the minds, the character, nor the wish to govern themselves. If that is true of you and of me, then the dictators are right. The truth will prevail, and the victory over dictatorship is won, not by guns and bombs, but by the proof that America has given and can continue to give, that Americans triumphantly carry the responsibilities of freedom.

Let us be strong enough, cool enough, vigilant and ceaselessly persevering enough to keep freedom and peace on that part of the earth that is ours to guard, and to hold good will in our hearts for all humanity.

Rose Wilder Lane Says . . . "Force Won't Keep the Peace"

(*Woman's Day*, February 1945)

Clearly, Lane did not get her wish that the United States would remain neutral during World War II. The United States entered the war following the bombing of Pearl Harbor, Hawaii, on December 7, 1941. During the war years, Lane became even more vocal about her point of view that American freedom meant freedom from government interference. She refused a Social

Security number, refused ration books, and raised her own produce to eat and sell during the war years. Lane also started her association with the National Economic Council's Review, *contributing articles as early as 1943. Her fiction career was over, and her most forceful political treatise,* The Discovery of Freedom, *was published in 1943. The book drew some acclaim, and today remains a focal point of libertarian thought as expressed by such groups as the Libertarian Party, the Cato Institute, and the Freedom Forum, all of which have Web sites that praise Lane's work and highlight her significance to their causes.*

This article, published in 1945, continues her conversation with Woman's Day *readers about war and the needs and desires of American citizens.*

Americans want no more war. We do not have the ancient delusion that a country or a group of persons can profit from war. We have never held the atrocious barbarian belief, still expressed in Europe and Asia, that war is the supreme spiritual act, the bloody human sacrifice that satisfies the gods and revives a nation's soul. We repudiate that pagan lie.

We know what war is. We will do anything to prevent any more of it. If permanent compulsory military service will even help to prevent war, we will accept that.

We want peace at any cost. Let us be honest; we wish for a peaceful world, but we pray for peace at home again. That is what we deeply want. That is a great deal to want; it is more than any other people have hoped for, and we Americans have had it.

Perhaps we do not think enough about that fact. It may seem childish to recall facts that we learned in school, but as children we did not think about them; as citizens we must think about plain facts.

Governments have been waging war during 2,800 of the past 3,000 years; peace has been an interval of about one year in fifteen. Gangsters in castle-forts, living by armed robbery, made the European States by armed force and oppression; war is their basis, and European statesmen inherit the wrongs of war and the task of making war. To their subjects, freed from serfdom only during the last century, war and poverty still seem as inevitable as death.

Only eight score years ago, Americans made a new kind of government unknown on earth before. They founded our government, not upon brutal force, but as John Quincy Adams said, upon "the moral and physical nature of man," upon the self-evident fact that God does not create rulers and subjects, but human beings, to each of whom He gives freedom to choose between right and wrong, self-control, and responsibility—in one word: liberty. They did this to insure for us, their posterity, "the blessings of liberty."

One of these blessings is peace. Our United States holds the world's all-time peace record: 33 years (1866–1898) of peace. In history's 6,000 years, no other strong Power, able to make war, has kept its peace for 33 years.

Two other blessings of liberty are material progress and prosperity. In one century, free men changed a barren wilderness into a land of abundance for the most prosperous people in history. Americans gave the world steamships, transoceanic cables, telephones, electric power, airplanes, modern medicine and surgery and sanitation. Since 1920, all governments except the British have looked to America for their countries' material development. In response, Americans industrialized Russia. Americans rationalized German industries, Americans modernized Japan and began to modernize China, Persia, Arabia, Africa, the whole earth.

Now we live in a new world. Nothing like this was ever before imagined; we hardly begin to understand it. Free men create a world that abolishes all the old barriers between human beings. This new world ignores races, creeds, classes, nations; it conquers space and time; it links together all persons on this planet.

Yesterday we wore silk stockings because Japanese women worked patiently with tiny insects' eggs; we ate pineapple ripened in Hawaii's sunshine because little Burmese men mined tin; we rode on air because turbaned Malays slashed into steamy jungles to make space for rubber trees; we smoked fine blends of tobacco because Greeks tended fields in Thessaly; and all these people shared the fruits of our work, as we shared theirs.

Free persons make a world that can exist only in peace; it cannot survive wars. The car in the garage tells us that, and the grocer's empty shelves.

We have learned, too, that this new world links all mankind together such that governments can no longer make limited wars. War is world war now; peace must be world peace. There is no other choice. If permanent compulsory military service in our country will help to keep all governments from making war, then we want it.

The question is merely a question of method. Is permanent compulsory service a method that prevents war? Is it a method that a government can use to keep world peace?

I do not think so. The arguments for this method were reactionary in Europe in 1797. They are not realistic in these United States of America in 1945. And if actions speak louder than words, the advocates of this method know that it will not stand examination by the common sense of the American people. If their proposal is sensible and right, why are they not hurrying to push it though Congress, quickly, before we can think about it? And before our fighting men come home?

We have an army now. No one expects another war the instant this one is ended. What conceivable reason requires this headlong rush to change the very basis of American life?

One thing is certain: When our sons come home, they will be realists. They will have no illusions about the wide world nor about our country's place in it. Does anyone dare to make any sacrifice for permanent peace? Then why this haste to fasten permanent conscription upon their infant sons—in their absence?

The advocates of this method say that strong military power can keep peace "by preventing aggression." Let us say in plain words what everybody knows: Nothing but a threat of war can prevent any war-making government from waging war. Nothing but war can stop a war.

Their actual proposal is this: Make these United States a strong military Power always so ready to fight that it can bully the whole world and prevent war merely by threatening to make war, in the hope that no other strong military Power will ever call the bluff. They add: Of course, an American representing whatever Administration may be in Washington must have the power to use American conscripts anywhere on earth, quickly, "to stop aggression," without consulting *our* representatives in Congress.

And what are our sons doing now, but "stopping aggression"?

Even this proposal assumes, mistakenly or falsely, that permanent, universal, compulsory military service makes a strong military power. It does not. On its record, it destroys a strong military Power.

In 1797, permanent compulsory military service was instituted in France by the reactionaries who defeated the first French revolution and paved the way for Napoleon, the Hitler of his time. For ten years, it gave Napoleon so much military power that, as he told Metternich, he "could afford to expend 3,000 men a month." It exhausted France, and caused

Napoleon's collapse. The French have had compulsory military service ever since, and have never had military strength enough to win another war.

For half a century, the French government has used permanent compulsory military service, and alliances with other Powers also having compulsory military purpose—to keep peace in Europe.

Do Americans want to copy the method of keeping peace which the French have used since 1871?

The Prussians adopted permanent conscription from Napoleon. Also, in 1866, they introduced to the Continent the American-British breech-loading rifle. The combination was terrific. Thoroughly drilled soldiers, loading, aiming, firing hundreds of breech-loading rifles as one automatic unit, had such terrible fire-power that it is still a proverb in Europe. It made Prussia the strongest Continental Power. Within eight years (1863–1871) Prussia won three great wars and founded modern Germany. The Germans have had permanent compulsory military service ever since—and have never won another war.

Meanwhile, Europeans flocked to our United States to escape from compulsory military service. More free than men have ever been elsewhere, they developed here the terrific productive energy, the mass-production and mass-distribution techniques, and the actual machines—trucks, tractors, planes—that have changed the Old World's wars.

Americans are about 1/15th of the world's population, on 1/17th of its land. Today we supply military power to all United Nations; we have mechanized the Russian armies, we are mechanizing Chinese armies, and we add the fighting force that tips the balance to victory in this war. Our country is the strongest military Power on earth.

Do these facts suggest that our generation of Americans should cynically break the promise that America has held for the whole world for 155 years, that we should think nothing of that moral obligation, abandon our own new way of life and its hope for the world's future—merely to desert our own military method for a method that has failed before our eyes in Europe?

Immorality is not practical, and it is immoral to offer freedom to all men and then give, to those who accept the offer, the very tyranny from which we promised them refuge. But the advocates of permanent military conscription do not base their arguments on morality, as indeed they could not. And on their own ground of unmoral expediency, their argument is absurd.

It is fantastic that the Nazi's foolish bragging still deludes any American so that he says, "America must never again be so unprepared for war." Who was prepared for this war?

France, Italy, Germany, Russia and Japan have had compulsory military service for generations. The Germans were on the Volga before "unprepared" England and "unprepared" America could get help to the Russians. Do we want a foreign aggressor pushing to the Mississippi? And who would help us then? Do we wish to be prepared for war as our enemies were prepared for this one? Would it not be sensible to imitate the victors in this war?

As Stalin said at Tehran, Capitalist production is winning this war. Today and in the future, the strongest military Power is the people having the greatest productive energy. That energy is manpower. It is the eager minds, the enterprise, inventiveness, profit-motive, skills, of self-controlling, self-reliant, free men. It comes from our boys who take the radio to pieces, wire our door knobs for sound, tinker with old jalopies, and clamor to get out of school into work they want to do.

Can any sensible person believe that a steady peacetime drain of millions of man-power years of that young energy, every year, from American industry into army camps, will not reduce America's productive energy and check the industrial progress which, alone, can hold our country's place as the strongest military Power on earth?

Our enemies fail, not only for lack of productive energy, but for lack of free men. Too late for them, the German and Japanese Generals discovered that the tools that free men make—trucks, tractors, bull-dozers, planes—require free wills to run them. In 1940, they were trying to drill their soldiers in self-reliance, independence, personal initiative and responsibility. No man can be compelled to act of his own free will.

Ortega y Gasset wisely says, "It must be emphasized that the warrior spirit is one thing, and the soldier spirit quite another. The soldier spirit (is) the degeneration of the warrior." Permanent conscription made soldiers of our enemies. Englishmen and Americans are warriors, free men who—when they must—fight for a cause they support and the truth they know.

From the halls of Montezuma to the shores of Tripoli, from Fort Duquesne to Aachen and Metz, the "well-trained" conscript-soldiers have never stood against Americans.

Certainly, conditions have changed now; Americans have changed them. Is that a reason that we should stop changing them, and begin now to imitate the failures of the Old World?

We Americans have our own military system, written into our Federal Constitution in the second provision of the Bill of Rights. Once before in history this system was used; it spread Roman law and the Roman peace over the known world. In our peaceful prosperity, our politicians have neglected it and our European-minded talkers have forgotten it, but it exists, in our State troops, our National Guard, our R.O.T.C. and our private military schools, and our volunteer regiments, and our peacetime army and navy and air force.

I think our own military system should be, and will be, modernized and revitalized by the knowledge and realism our sons will bring home with them; and it should be vigorously maintained by a Congress and a War Department wide awake to our country's constant world responsibility, and relying once more upon the energy, the organizing ability, the competitive and co-operative spirit, and the sound idealism of a free people.

These stopped aggression when fewer than three million Americans faced on our own soil the conscript-soldiers of the strongest European power, when aggressors held our cities and burned our Capitol in Washington. If America's warrior spirit is not doped to sleep by lies and suppressed by permanent conscription, Americans will resist tyranny and fight for liberty anywhere on this earth, as willingly as they went to war to free the Cubans forty-six years ago.

Americans began, and never abandoned, the world revolution for limited government, for personal freedom and human rights. And from the days when Jefferson advised Lafayette during the first French revolution of 1789, until Homer Lea taught Sun Yat Sen to lead the Chinese revolution of 1911, our country has inspired and Americans have led the attack upon tyranny around this earth. In history and in the world now, Americans stand for law, for human rights, for the liberty and dignity of man.

It is not a little thing, actually, to change government and human society on this earth. That is not done in a century and a half; it will not be done soon. Against the weight of nearly all past history, against the survivals and revivals of pagan beliefs that support old and new tyrannies, Americans must lead the struggle for liberty and law until free men make a new world, not only of material abundance, but also of freedom and justice.

So long as tyranny exists, tyrants will make war. There is only one way to make permanent world peace: restrict every government to the simple duty of protecting the life, liberty and property of all peaceful persons from the few criminals among them. So long as the people of any large nation believe the rulers can control their lives, their work, and their property, and provide for their welfare, they will obey tyrants, and the tyrants will make a war. Bastiat said truly, "When men and goods cannot cross frontiers, soldiers will."

Permanent world peace cannot follow this war. Too many tyrannies will exist. Too many persons still cherish the delusions that create tyranny. One of these delusions is the belief that a regimented and conscripted people as a strong military Power, or Powers, can keep peace by military force. Freedom makes peace; nothing but freedom and justice on earth can make an enduring world peace. Freedom must be defended so long as tyranny exists, and only free people can defend freedom.

7.
Mrs. Lane Writes from the Heartland

In addition to the opinion pieces, Lane's material from Woman's Day *also focuses on storytelling. Lane's favorite subjects at this time were American; her favorite themes were hard work, perseverance, independence, and freedom. These themes are readily apparent in her political works, such as* Discovery of Freedom; *they are also apparent in the "Little House" books, which she edited. They are no less obvious in the following stories. But in these pieces, Lane falls back on her ability to tell stories through the use of vivid description and witty dialogue. In her hands, these features become works of art that offer readers a glimpse of American life on the home front during the war period.*

We Go to a Wedding

(*Woman's Day,* June 1940)

The first piece of this section was not bylined in the magazine; however, it is listed as one of Lane's pieces in the Woman's Day *records. It is possible that Lane, who was building a reputation as a political rhetorician, preferred not to have her name associated with what almost certainly was viewed as a "fluff" feature. However, the style speaks for itself; Lane's gift for putting readers in the moment through one absolute point of view—in this case, the guest's point of view—allows those who read this piece to attend the wedding of this young couple and share in their joy. It was written for June publication, at the heart of the traditional wedding season, and offers a valuable look at mainstream American social life in 1940.*

It was the most beautiful wedding. The invitations read: Mr. and Mrs. Richard Hagemann request the honor of your presence at the marriage of their daughter Edith Anna Margaret to Mr. John Alexander Grant, junior—

Six years ago, on the summer day when the Hagemanns were moving into the small house of their own that they had just bought in Tarrytown, a little girl crossed the street to look at Edith. The fourteen-year-olds were talking when a sixteen-year-old boy came along. His name was Johnny Grant, but everyone called him Buddy.

After supper that evening, Edith and Johnny were out with the other boys and girls of the neighborhood, playing hide-and-seek, up and down the tree-lined street.

That was the beginning. Nearly all Americans have known what followed, though each of us cherishes memories like no others. There were school days, then high school days, tournaments and cheering squads, picnics and parties. Buddy saved dimes to take Edith to the movie on Saturday night. After the movie they were in the row perched on stools in the favorite drugstore, drinking sodas, eating chocolate-marshmallow-banana-nut sundaes, all talking at once.

There was the day that Buddy got his first car, the little old much-used coupe that they will never forget. And there was the afternoon when Edith's very best friend lured a willing Buddy into Edith's house, leaving Edith with the lawn to mow. That whole afternoon those two sat talking on the cold radiator in the window, their backs indifferent to Edith, while under the hot sun she furiously pushed the lawn mower, vowing never to go anywhere with Buddy again, never as long as she lived!

There were plenty of other boys. She had plenty to do without them. She was busy in school and Sunday school, and studying music, helping her mother in house and garden, having good times. She was merry and friendly and popular, and when she was sixteen no one thought of her without thinking of Buddy.

An attachment so early worries parents. Edith's father and mother like Buddy, but they decided that her mother would speak to them. One day she did. She told them that they were too young to be together so much, that Edith should spend more time with other boys, and Buddy with other girls.

They admitted that she was right, and Buddy reluctantly agreed that Edith might do that, but he did not see how he could. He said, "The trouble is, I'm not interested in any girl but Edith."

He finished high school that spring and went to work in a gas station. Then Edith graduated and commuted to a business school in New York. Then she was commuting to a job in a New York office. And she was following her mother's good advice.

Johnny Grant says that persuading her was the hardest work he ever did. But she laughs at him. "You never did persuade me! I just made up my mind."

So they were engaged, and why should they wait to be married? She is twenty now and she has a job; he is twenty-two and he also has a job. He sends out the delivery trucks for an oil company. There is not much money, but ever since he saved to take her to the movies they have known how to get the most from a little money and how to have plenty of good times that don't cost a penny.

They were hunting a nice apartment that they could afford, when her parents thought of making one in their house. Two upstairs rooms, with large closet and bath, could be cut off to make a separate apartment. Edith and Buddy joined the planning, liking the idea.

They shopped for rugs and curtains, a davenport and chairs. Edith can cook in her mother's kitchen; for parties the dining room will be hers. Mr. Hagemann cut a door through a wall to give their apartment its own private balcony. Downstairs by the front door he set a second doorbell that will ring for Mr. and Mrs. John Grant.

Friends were giving showers for Edith, wedding presents were pouring in, neighbors offered to help with the Easter wedding. In February Miss Anthony baked Edith's wedding cake. Dark, rich, spicy and full of fruit, it was ripening its flavors.

Mrs. Souvaine was planning the clothes. The bride's gown and veil, frocks and hats for the maid of honor, the bridesmaids, the flower girls, must all be chosen, fitted, finished and delivered in four weeks, and Edith had only minutes snatched from lunch hours. For the Easter wedding she chose the earliest springtime colors, pale green and yellow. And in the hurry everything almost went wrong, even to the nearly-last-minute delivery of the bridesmaids' hoopskirted frocks—without hoops.

Four days before the wedding, the meats were boiling in *Woman's Day's* kitchen to make chicken paté squares for fifty guests. Two days before, the paté was in its boxes of bread, Miss Anthony was frosting the wedding cake and editors were busily wrapping slices for guests to take home to dream on. Miss Anthony had a happy idea. One wedding cake she decorated with toasted almonds, candied cherries and angelica (frosting would yellow) and she wrapped it in brandied cloths and shut it into a tight tin box, a present for the Grants' first wedding anniversary.

The day before the wedding Miss Anthony attended to every detail of the wedding supper. The tiny cream puffs waited to be filled, the salad dressing was made for the chicken paté squares. Every knife was sharpened. In the church rooms Miss Anthony counted plates and cups, silver and glassware. She assembled tablecloths, napkins, punch bowls and vases. She ordered white and yellow tulips, daisies and snapdragons, and did not forget huckleberry leaves to screen the Sunday school blackboard. She saw the rows of chairs folded and stacked away, and the floor well waxed for dancing. She hired the janitor's two sons to wait on table.

She went to bed satisfied that nothing was overlooked. In the night she woke suddenly, remembering that she had all those chairs solidly stacked in front of the cupboard that held the dishes.

Mrs. Souvaine, however, had got the bridesmaids' hoops to Tarrytown. And punctually the sun rose on the wedding day.

That afternoon the guests began to arrive at the white Colonial church. Ushers led us through soft organ music to the pews. Behind the scenes the tip-toe janitor stealthily moved the chairs, and the bridegroom waited with the best man. In the church kitchen Miss Anthony's staff was filling cream puffs and spreading salad dressing. White jackets for the janitor's boys were there, but not the janitor's boys. By the altar lighted with Easter lilies, the choir's soloist beautifully sang, "I love you truly, truly, dear."

Photographers waited, chilly, on the church steps. In front of the Hagemanns' house the bridal party confronted the problem of hoopskirts in cars. Edith's father helped the glimmering bride into his own car and took the wheel beside her.

The church was full. An usher escorted Mr. and Mrs. Grant to their correct places. Another escorted Mrs. Hagemann, rather breathless and very pretty in the blue lace and blue hat. Then triumphantly the music said that the bride was coming.

Up the aisle the ushers passed, but who saw them? The bridesmaids came in pale green organza, crownless hats like halos around dusky hair, and slender bodices graceful above the wide, ruffled hoopskirts. Then the maid of honor, like spring sunshine, haloed slenderness in billowing skirts. Then two of Edith's little Sunday school pupils, small girls very serious and darling in little yellow bonnets and long yellow dresses, carefully strewing forsythia blossoms from baskets on their bare, plump arms. Then the bride. She was beautiful.

She was more than beautiful; she was at home. You knew that many, many times, since she was a child, she had come up this aisle with her father and had seen these friends here. You knew that faith in goodness was as natural to her as air.

An old lady who loves her, having no daughter of her own to wear a bridal veil, gave Edith the heirloom of old white Spanish lace made long ago for a bride. Such lace is no longer made nor worn. Edith had the precious gift set into her wedding veil. It covered her dark hair and shone amid the yards of filmy net following her gleaming gown up the aisle. She stood with Buddy before the minister, between ranks of Easter lilies.

Everyone heard their voices, serious but not shaken or tense, "—to have and to hold, to love, cherish and honor, for better or worse, in sickness and in health, and forsaking all others I will keep only unto thee, so long as we both shall live."

They came happily down the aisle together. They were to receive congratulations in the reception room, but friends overtook them in the church, each with a personal word to say while kissing Edith and shaking Johnny's hand, and each was warmly answered. Only the anguished photographers formed the correct reception line, after all congratulations had been said, and the orchestra was singing with all its might, "Oh, Johnny! Oh, Johnny! How can you love!"

"Let me call you sweetheart," the music confidently implored while the bridal party settled at the table clothed in white lace. Those janitor's boys simply had not come. Miss Anthony and her staff served the bridal party and presided at punch bowls and buffet. Everyone was having the most marvelous time.

The food was delicious and so pretty. Chicken paté squares in white rims edged with green and with yellow, golden bubbles of cheese-filled cream puffs, tiny rolled sandwiches, olives, curled celery and raw carrot sticks, made a picture on a plate, a picture rapidly vanishing.

More sandwiches went begging. Small boys invaded the kitchen to snitch more carrot sticks. "And 'twas there that Annie Laurie gave me her promise true. Gave me her promise true," the orchestra exulted.

A secret dismay agitated the kitchen; the ice cream had not come. But no one missed it. The bride was opening the dance.

Away on waves of the "Blue Danube" her husband swept her shining in mists of veil. Her father cut in. Johnny brought out his mother. But his father had taken Edith now, and again her father cut out Johnny. Then Johnny began to dance with her mother, but now the best man had claimed Edith and once more her father tapped Johnny's shoulder. Pursued by laughter, Johnny had to yield to Mr. Hagemann, in turn the maid of honor and each bridesmaid. Of the whole bridal party, only Johnny had none of that dance; when he reached his laughing bride again, the waltz ended.

Now the dance was in full swing, the floor filled. Every moment the bride's partners changed; she was the center, the queen. Hardly anyone noticed when she and Johnny were dancing together, she would hold out her hand and draw a bashful youth from his corner. When someone cut in, she would hand him over to a wall-flower girl before she left him. The most beautiful thing at Edith's wedding party was her grace giving everyone a happy time there. Once dancing quietly with her, her husband kissed her cheek.

The ice cream came. It was brick ice cream, yellow, white and green. And there was plenty of wedding cake, though one avid child was risking dreadful nightmares.

At eight o'clock the orchestra leader's signals were melting the dancing couples in circling lines. Grand-right-and-left, and break into couples again. At half past eight, when the long lines were circling, the music changed to "Auld Lang Syne." Impromptu, Edith and Johnny went arm-in-arm inside the circle, saying good-bys. Near the door they broke through the ring. A blizzard of confetti was barely quick enough to swirl after them. They were gone.

Only their families followed Johnny's fleeing car to Edith's home, where she dressed for the wedding journey.

Someone said, "Edith's mother must have been beautiful at her wedding, too."

"Oh, she was," Mr. Hagemann said fervently. "And she has always been good to have in the house."

"I had a beautiful wedding." Mrs. Hagemann remembered. "I always hoped that Edith would have a wedding as lovely as mine. Now she has had one even more beautiful."

Calm in the dish-clattering kitchen, Miss Anthony gathered up the fragments. "Thank goodness," she said, "the ice cream came."

Minnesota Farm Boy

(*Woman's Day,* July 1940)

This article, which did carry Lane's byline, tells the story of Minnesota's Harold Stassen, who at that time was the youngest governor in the United States. In telling his story, Lane speaks not to the governor himself, but to his parents, focusing on how their son epitomized American values as Lane viewed them. She writes, again, from the first person, but she chooses to let her subjects tell their story through dialogue and action, bringing to bear the literary techniques that enrich her work. It again provides a look at rural midwestern values and life in 1940.

In reading this piece, one is tempted to wonder if Lane is really discussing her own parents' lives and values.

He's got a reputation for horse-sense and he's the youngest Governor in the United States. Elected at the age of 31 in 1938, to head the State of Minnesota, Harold E. Stassen has been chosen to make the keynote speech at the Republican National Convention this year.

Years of drought made the western wheatlands an arid desert scoured by dust storms. A million farmers were homeless when banks foreclosed the mortgages. But mortgages were frozen assets and the banks failed, ruining depositors. The Middle West was overrun by homeless families desperately hunting work. This was the news of the 1890's.

Only a few people in one small town knew that, in the worst of those times, Elsie Jansen married William Stassen. When she said she would marry him, William Stassen arranged to buy a small piece of his parents' farm, and on it he built a one-room house, with an attic and a lean-to.

They have lived there ever since. The other day I went there to see them. The house is six miles from the air-conditioned Capitol building in St. Paul, where their son, Harold, works in the Governor's office. Their son, Harold, is the Governor. Elected when he was 31 years old, by one of the largest votes ever cast in Minnesota, he is the youngest Governor in the United States.

The house is still a farmhouse. Beside it is the truck garden, and meadows stretch beyond the barn. A flower garden borders the lawn, old box elders and an enormous poplar shade it, and hollyhocks were blooming against the gray-shingled walls of the house when I knocked at the screen door.

Mrs. Stassen, in a print dress and crisp bib-apron, came to open it. Her white hair was combed back to a small knot at the neck, and her face was weathered by sun and wind. She had just finished picking tomatoes for market, she said. Mr. Stassen was haying. You can't stop to pick garden truck when the hay is down and a sudden rain may spoil it.

It is an achievement to be the mother of a son who does so much before he is 32. I wanted to hear Mrs. Stassen's ideas on bringing up children. But she seemed to have none. She said that not one of the children had caused any real worry. Harold, she said, had always been bright. "He took to books," she said. He graduated from high school when he was 15, and worked his way through the university and got his law degree before he was 21. He sold fruit and vegetables from a highway stand to make his spending money in high school, and in the university he worked in a bakery and ran an adding machine, and Mrs. Stassen didn't remember what all he did, until he worked as sleeping-car conductor on the Chicago run.

"I did worry some about that," she said. "There for two years he didn't get enough sleep. But he said he used the time studying. He said it wouldn't hurt him to lose some sleep, and now I guess it didn't. Yes, he's done well; he's a good boy, and bright. All our boys are good boys and doing well according to the abilities the Lord gave them."

William is a sheet-metal worker. Elmer owns a small grocery in South St. Paul, and Arthur, the youngest, delivered milk until he passed civil service examinations and got a job in the state highway department. Mrs.

Stassen showed me their photographs on the walls and on the piano, pictures of Violet, the youngest Stassen, who is married now and living in St. Paul, and the pictures of her seven grandchildren.

There is something in the atmosphere of an old farmhouse that no decorator could reproduce. The living room is quiet and calm, and nobody does anything there. It is a room that a woman cleans and polishes scrupulously every day for years and on Sundays and in the evenings after supper, her husband and the children sit there not saying much. If neighbors come in, there is still not much to say. They sit relaxed after their muscular work in sun and air, glad to be sheltered, and pleased that the chores are done, the stock fed and bedded, the crops planted or harvested. They wish for rain or sunshine but they know that the weather will be what it will be and that only God can temper the wind to the shorn lamb. Though the lamps are lighted, they feel in their marrow the earth's bulk increasing between them and the sun; they feel the deepening night, and they think of the sunlight's swift return to the eastern sky; they remember that tomorrow is another day of work. So they go yawning to bed.

I said to Mrs. Stassen, "I like your house."

"It's just grown," she said, her pleasure in it shining from her face as transparent as a child's. "The first room we had is the kitchen now, and we boarded up the lean-to for a pantry. We kept adding. Folks used to laugh; they said whenever a new baby was coming there was Mr. Stassen building onto the house. The dining room was the parlor as long as the children were little, but when they began growing up we built on this whole front to make room for parties."

I leaped at this. "You were making their home attractive, you wanted it to be the social center where they'd bring their friends, instead of being away in the evenings—"

Mrs. Stassen looked completely baffled. Obviously she had never heard of such a thought. She said feebly, "Why, we wanted them to have good times."

"You've brought up five children and they've all turned out well," I said. "You must have something to say about bringing up children. What is it?"

"They must mind," she said instantly and emphatically, and in the same breath, "our children had religious training always. From the time they were babies we took them with us to Sunday school and church; they just grew up in the church."

I should have known it; the house told me, and every word and look of Mrs. Stassen's, that one thing she wanted in her children was goodness. The Stassens brought up their children to be good, according to the Ten Commandments and the teachings of Christ. And if they ever heard psychologists, the Stassens would have dismissed them as the crackling of thorns under a pot.

We went through the dining room into a perfect kitchen. There is a polished wood range surrounded by cupboards and shelves. Uncrowded on the linoleum floor stands an oilcloth-covered table large enough to seat eight, with chairs ranged around it. Mrs. Stassen showed me her ample pantry, and I said, "Don't you detest these narrow streamlined, scientific kitchens that are like laboratories?"

The Governor's mother was completely surprised. "I don't know," she said. "I never saw one. Are there kitchens like that?"

Mr. Stassen came into the house for a drink, dusty and hot from the hay field, and Mrs. Stassen fetched glasses of ginger beer from the icebox. We talked about Harold's boyhood, and his father told me that Harold had been summoned to court when he was ten, to give evidence in a trial for theft. Harold had seen the man stealing, and the lawyer could not shake his testimony. "The lawyers and the law and the court fascinated him," his father said. "Harold always liked to argue. He said that day, on our way home, he wanted to be a lawyer."

I asked him for his ideas about bringing up children, and he said thoughtfully, "Well, one thing's important. We talked it over beforehand, my wife and I, and agreed that we would always stand together. We'd try to agree 50–50, but if something came up that we couldn't, then it would be 49–51 and I'd—well, I'd be the 51. Afterward we'd talk it over by ourselves and maybe argue it out to an agreement, but in front of the children there'd never be any argument. The children always knew that their mother and me, we stood together."

We always enjoy talking about our children. But always, when I spoke of the Governor today, his mother's eyes stopped smiling. I asked her finally, "Aren't you proud of him?"

She was distressed. "Yes," she said honestly. "And we're glad he is doing what he set out to do. But it's hard on him. Being Governor is hard. It's hard to be sure what's right, when so many folks are pushing and pulling and arguing, and it's hard to do what's right, so many are against it."

"But think how much good a Governor can do," I said.

"Yes," she admitted. "But it's hard on Harold. I don't say I'm against his being Governor; that's what he wants to do. And I don't doubt he'll do what's right. But I can't help thinking how hard it is on him. And he must make so many enemies."

"He'll be all right," Mr. Stassen said. "He's a good boy, and he always was bright."

8.
Mrs. Lane's Final Work

Between 1945 and 1960, Lane was busy with a number of projects, even as she considered herself "retired." From 1945 to 1950, she edited the National Economic Council's Review of Books, *and reams of letters flowed from her typewriter to correspondents as varied as Dorothy Thompson, Jasper Crane, and J. Edgar Hoover. A Federal Bureau of Investigation file on Lane, available in the Hoover Presidential Library archives, tells of her interactions with that organization. Apparently, Lane had written a negative opinion about the FBI on the back of a postcard in early 1942; flagged by a postal worker, it drew the attention of FBI agents, who arrived on her doorstep to question her about it.*

This incident inspired Lane to write the story up for a pamphlet she published called "What Is This, the Gestapo?" That action did not endear her to the FBI or to Hoover, and the correspondence carried on. One agent dismissed Lane's claims of harassment by the FBI. Special Agent D. K. Brown told Hoover that he didn't think Lane's claims had merit. "It appears to me that the Lane woman is a sensationalist and a publicity seeker, who seized upon a minor and unimportant incident to gain nationwide publicity," Brown wrote in 1943.[1]

Lane also continued writing for Woman's Day, *crafting a set of articles about needlework that she intended to use to educate American women*

1. D. K. Brown to J. Edgar Hoover, August 16, 1943; RWLP, FBI file, box 5.

about their unique roles in American history. "I am running a really Right Wing Extremist series of articles on needlework in Woman's Day; *Eileen Tighe, that editor, has always been WITH us," Lane wrote to Jasper Crane in 1962. "And the reader response is terrific; astounding; tens of thousands of letters saying, Thank you, THANK you, for American history, American spirit."*[2] *In these pieces, Lane elaborated on her favorite themes of American individualism and freedom from government interference, while focusing on a determined thesis that the history of such thought can be traced through the history of American needlework. Together with specific stitches and patterns, Lane pieced together an American history that placed women and women's work at the forefront of American individualist thought. She also reflected in places about her family's history.*

Her family had, by this time, been immortalized through the "Little House" series of books. Her father, Almanzo Wilder, died in 1949, but he lived on through collective memory as the young farm boy in upstate New York and the daring young pioneer who had saved an entire town from starvation in 1881, as depicted in the series. Her mother, Laura Ingalls Wilder, died in 1957, with Lane at her side, having secured the memory of her pioneering family in American culture for posterity. Both women drew on that collective memory in their work, but Lane carried the banner forward through the needlework series, which was collected and published as Woman's Day Book of American Needlework *in 1963, and through her custodianship of the "Little House" series, to which she added new texts. Lane wrote a foreword and introduction to her mother's diary of the trip the family had made from South Dakota to Missouri in 1892 and published it as* On the Way Home. *She also ensured that custodianship of the Ingalls-Wilder-Lane memory would be continued under the auspices of her heir, another informally adopted "grandson," Roger Lea MacBride.*

In 1965, the needlework book finished, Woman's Day *editors asked Lane if she would consider traveling to Vietnam and writing about her experience there. The Department of Defense wanted a reporter to go and tell the story of what was happening in Vietnam from the "woman's perspective" and contacted* Woman's Day *to take on the task. The difficulty Lane had in getting this story is told in a special, short feature opposite the index in*

2. RWL to Jasper Crane, February 21, 1962; reprinted in *The Lady and the Tycoon,* 285.

the December 1965 issue of Woman's Day. *Lane, who was always ready to take on a new adventure, was nearly kept from going by government officials who discovered her age. She was seventy-eight, and she left anyway.*

"August in Viet Nam" appeared in Woman's Day *in December 1965, and it capped a lengthy career while making clear that Lane's primary life's interests—Americanism, freedom, total independence—still had a significant place in her life. It stands not only as a pivotal closing chapter in her career, but also as a commentary on a conflict and country that had a lasting effect on the American psyche. Three years later,* Woman's Day *asked her to go around the world, reporting on global conditions from her unique perspective. She died in her sleep the night before she was to leave. "August in Viet Nam" was the last piece she published, and it is a fitting capstone for the life she led and the principles she held.*

August in Viet Nam

(*Woman's Day,* December 1965)

No land on earth is more beautiful than Viet Nam. The central mountain peaks climb blue beyond blue above dense forests and cleared slopes where hamlets cluster in villages and streams run swiftly. Below them the South China Sea thrusts deep harbors between jungle-covered mountains reflected, dark green, in the clear water.

One harbor curves half around Qui Nhon, the capital of Binh Dinh province, a mass of thatched cottages, churches, pagodas, and pastel-covered buildings with red tiled roofs and many balconies. Bicyclists bump along the cobbled streets among peasants in conical hats and black shorts, balancing loads dangling from the ends of shoulder-yokes.

Twenty-five years ago the French bombed rebels in Qui Nhon. Then Americans bombed the Japanese in Qui Nhon. Then the French, returning, bombed the rebels out of Qui Nhon. But the League for the Independence of Viet Nam fought on, eight years longer, till independence was won at Dien Bien Phu in 1954.

Diplomats of 16 nations met in Switzerland to make the peace; the United States took no part in that conference. The peace terms proved that Ho Chi Minh was right; he had insisted that Communists gain more from negotiating than fighting.

Ho Chi Minh is not the man's name. He was Nguyen Van Cung when he left his native village. In Paris in 1920 when he founded the French section of Lenin's Third Communist International, he called himself Nguyen Ai Quoc. In 1941 when Moscow sent him into China he was a toughened and wily Communist agent, but Chiang Kai-shek knew Communists and jailed him. Two years later, released to command the seizure of his own country, he took the name Ho Chi Minh to hide his identity from men who had spent their lives working for Viet Nam's independence. He gathered them with Communists into the League for the Independence of Viet Nam, called for short Viet Minh. While together they fought the returning French armies, the Communists tried to control the Viet Minh and in the turmoil of victory, naturally, as Communists did everywhere in Europe, they killed the patriots who had resisted their control. Ho Chi Minh's storm troopers seized Hanoi and eliminated his opponents there. But he made the Communist bands in the south stop killing, bury their arms, be quiet while the diplomats talked.

In Geneva the diplomats gave him Hanoi with the Red River valley, its seaports and some 14 millions of the Viet people—even after hundreds of thousands had fled south to escape him. More than that: the peace terms dictated a "free election" which certainly would give him all Viet Nam, since he had in his absolute power more than half the voters and held under his orders the armed bands scattered through the south.

The south's two-year-old government refused to hold any such election. The United States were befriending the young government. The peace was uneasy.

Still it was peace and, as always, people began rebuilding. Peasants came to market in Qui Nhon's ruins; workers were clearing streets and filling bomb craters; thatchers were covering bamboo frames of cottages with palm fronds. Americans came; the United States Operations Mission (USOM) was bringing help in education, sanitation, public health; people waited in long lines for inoculations against cholera, typhus, smallpox. A new hotel, five stories tall, was finished; its ordinary hand-wrought ironwork, tiled floors, high ceilings, boasted modern air-conditioning, shower baths and in every bedroom a Western mattress-bed, as well as the usual hardwood slab to sleep on. All Americans being fabulously rich, as everyone knows, of course they lived in the hotel.

One night a terrific explosion jolted sleepers awake. They hurried outdoors. The hotel, all five stories, had collapsed into a screaming heap. A crowd attacked it, tugging, digging, shouting, prying, getting out bodies and men and women still alive. There was no hospital in Qui Nhon. Doctors gave morphine. The injured were laid carefully on makeshift stretchers and men carried them to the airport where there was one plane to take them to hospitals in Saigon. At the airport they walked into rifle fire.

They knew then that the hotel had been bombed. This was an attack on Qui Nhon. There were no troops. Nobody had weapons. The city's only defense was seven helicopters with light machine guns. Pilots got them into the air and kept them circling, holding back the attackers in the darkness all around and diverting their fire from the men loading stretchers into the plane. At first dawn when the plane took off, two large boats full of armed men were coming across the bay. The helicopters went out to meet them and hovering in swarms of bullets they sank one boat and drove back the other.

So Ho Chi Minh's men began the "War of Liberation" in Qui Nhon. When I was there recently that war was eight years old. For twenty-five years the people had been living in the midst of war. The site of the bombed hotel was bare but thatchers and masons were working on buildings and peasants were coming to market. Viet troops were in Qui Nhon. The Seventh Fleet cruised on the sea-horizon. Supply ships were unloading on the beach and Larks, those monster trucks on land and stubby boats at sea, were crawling up from the harbor and chugging away. But nobody went swimming or fishing on the bay. Communists, the Viet Cong, might be in the jungle on the other shore. Planes did not circle into the wind above Qui Nhon airport. They flew straight in or straight out to sea and turning north to Da Nang or south to Saigon, they kept out of range from the mountains. For a "War of Liberation" is stealthy, it is hidden subversion and secret invasion.

To know why 34 governments and many private agencies have men in South Viet Nam supporting and defending that young government, you must understand that a "War of Liberation" is a tactic in the world war that the Third Communist International declared in Moscow forty years ago: "We hereby formally declare war on the whole world by every means in our power, including force of arms."

This declaration, published world-wide in all major languages, is so monstrous and seemed so absurd then that few except Communists took it seriously. Do them justice: Communists truly believe that they must destroy us and everything we value, in order to make mankind be what they believe Mankind should be. For their faith they torture and kill; they suffer and die for it, too. A "War of Liberation" in jungles is untold misery, but it is a tactic tested and proved. It took Yugoslavia; it took Czechoslovakia. Country by country for three thousand miles it took Asia, from the Baltic to the Bering Sea; and China, North Korea, Tibet. It took Cuba. It took Indonesia.

Filipinos checked it in their islands; it halted in Malaya, Burma, Laos, Cambodia, waiting. If it takes strategic Viet Nam, then to be "liberated" are the Philippines, Australia, Hawaii. Hawaii?

When Ho Chi Minh could not take South Viet Nam by faking an election, the Communist bands in the south resumed killing their opponents. Tong Bo, the Council of Ho Chi Minh's People's Democratic Republic in Hanoi, sent trained assassins to help them. In 1959 they murdered 1,600 village chiefs serving as local officials of the southern government. Villagers stopped calling them Viet Minh and called them Viet Cong, a not-respectful term for Communist. Openly or stealthily the Viet Cong killed any leader who resisted them: Christian priests, Buddhist bonzes, teachers, notables. They killed the families of men who enlisted in the national army. On May 23, 1961, President Kennedy said that 4,000 had been murdered during 1960.

The Viet Cong were a few thousands among twelve and one-half millions, but they were organized, single-minded, and armed. One band of them outnumbered the armed defenders of any village, and no one knew where they would strike. They raided, took what they wanted, vanished. Or they asked for food and villagers gave it amiably, rather than die for a few measures of rice. Troupes of young singers, dancers, actors went from village to village; ardently deluded, they gave evening entertainments showing the heroic Viet Cong defeating the French and in future driving out the American imperialists.

Technically this is the first phase of a "War of Liberation." Adapted to conditions in the country attacked, it is a time, years or decades long, of infiltrating, eliminating opponents, weakening resistance, confusing, dividing, frightening, bribing, wearing down mental and moral strength.

The schoolteacher in Qui Nhon knew that the Viet Cong had sentenced him to death. He was taking some precautions but he still continued to teach the history of Viet Nam, patriotism and morality.

One morning the Viet Cong stopped a school bus. They told the driver to take the children home and not to drive them to school again. He took them home. But the Viets want schools. A bitter grievance against the French was a lack of schools; still they are not illiterate people. All village notables and many peasants read. More than once in the deafening, oven-hot military planes I have seen a Viet private, seat-belted into the swaying canvas loops called bucket seats, reading while his comrades slept. Children beg to go to school. Your own must not grow up ignorant. The Viet Cong might never return; they are here today and gone tomorrow.

Finally the parents risked it; the children went to school again. They went safely, one week, two weeks, part of a third. Then the Viet Cong stopped the bus.

They looked the children over, picked out a bright six-year-old and cut off her fingers. They told the children that worse would be done to them if they went to school again. They told the driver to take them home.

Such methods tend to make people docile. For eight years the Viet Cong used such methods through the length and breadth of free Viet Nam, until it was said that the government governed by day and the Viet Cong at night. Then in the monsoon season of 1965, in the highlands, suddenly they changed their ways.

They assaulted village after village, took it, rounded up the men and boys to take with them, and use as labor. They looted the village thoroughly, destroyed orchards and field and garden crops, burned the houses, and said to the women, "walk out."

Within weeks 300,000 women and children descended on Binh Dinh province. Among them were some from primitive mountain tribes, who are Vietnamese as Seminoles in the Everglades are Americans. There are some tens of thousands of these tribal people in the highlands. Each tribe has its own language, customs, religion and weapons. Several tribes are renowned for loyalty and courage, but their pictures in our newspapers do not accurately represent Viet soldiers.

These hundreds of thousands of helpless, homeless women were thrown on Qui Nhon as if living persons were a missile, a bomb. Qui Nhon's Buddhists, Catholics, Protestants, rallied from the shock and cared for their own in refugee camps, with help from national, provincial and local officials and USOM Americans. Gladys Philpott, USOM Teacher Education Advisor, was preparing to open schools for the refugee children and allotting textbooks from the 10,000,000 that she had printed in South Viet Nam, Japan, and Australia.

The Viet Cong were destroying their sources of supply, the villages. Were they going to risk the second phase of a "War of Liberation"—the armed attack, the sudden assault to smash a government and take power? It was known that regular troops of the North Viet Nam army had entered and were entering South Viet Nam; three divisions were said to be on the highlands. How many were under the jungle cover couldn't be known.

The Viet Cong "controlled," as people said, the countryside around Saigon and large areas farther south. They controlled the highlands from Qui Nhon to Pleiku to the Cambodian border, right across the middle of South Viet Nam. They "controlled" the country by controlling roads.

It isn't difficult to control a road. A few men do it. Now and then stop a truck and kill the driver. Stop a bus and kidnap whom you please. Soon no truck driver will use that road. Many persons will not use those buses. Then dicker with the lines, and you are bargaining for power, they are bargaining for life. People cannot live without trade; in cities and towns they must have food from the farmland, they must exchange goods for it. Roads are arteries of trade; to keep them open the owners of trucks and buses will pay tolls, drivers will obey orders.

So the Viet Cong controlled the land; the government held Saigon, the capital, and the capitals of the 43 provinces. On a map or in words the situation seemed disastrous. Politically the ten-year-old government was as shaky as the young United States had been for 26 years: 1789–1815. There were only 600,000 men in the government's armed forces; no more than barely enough to hold the cities, though in proportion to population they would be 9,000,000 in the United States. And 80 percent of them were volunteers.

In Saigon the public buildings, the embassies, and the huge official installations of American civilian workers were barricaded with concrete blocks and barbed wire and guarded by soldiers inspecting identity cards. Around them swirled the city, a torrent of some two million persons, any of whom could be Viet Cong dynamiters or assassins.

Saigon is a modern city. It has a cathedral, churches, pagodas, convents, colleges, hospitals, beautiful parks, fine restaurants and hotels, night clubs, arcades of enticing shops. The swarming slum-alleys and the closed-in dark markets are dirty, the cleaner streets and boulevards are whirlpools of bicycles, pedicabs, motorcycles, tiny taxis, military trucks, official cars and men, women, children nonchalant among them. In the evenings all is floodlighted from the tops of buildings.

Taller buildings were going up in every direction; one morning they stopped. Not a worker was on the girders in the sky. A strike? No; the Viet Cong ordered: No more sand into Saigon. Trucks were running but no driver would bring in a load of sand. Concrete requires sand; building was stopped until sand could be brought by sea.

This was a futile nuisance. How silly, I said; why do the Viet Cong do it? A Viet woman answered, lightly scornful, "They want us to know they're there." She meant: They so stupidly believe that we are stupid.

In a beautiful old Viet house in Saigon, Miss A. Elizabeth Brown heads the Viet staff of Foster Parents. You know Foster Parents: fifteen dollars a month cares for a child who needs you, who answers your letters and warms your heart. Miss Brown has 4,600 foster children and she isn't any longer giving them your Christmas presents. The railroad is destroyed, the Viet Cong control the roads, the planes have no space for parcels. Last year a helpful French priest was driving a caseworker to his village with presents for a hundred children. The Viet Cong stopped the car, took its load and kidnapped the priest.

Left on the road in a car she could not drive, the caseworker got on a bus to go back to Saigon. The road was mined. The bus was delayed into the night. Next morning the caseworker said to Miss Brown that the only thing she could think of, the whole time, was what would become of her four little children without her?

Miss Brown sends no more mothers out of Saigon. Letters and money orders go out by mail and only girls go to the villages to see the foster children. They wear peasants' black dress, travel on cheapest crowded buses and pray to meet no Viet Cong who know they work for Americans. Stupidly I asked one, "Aren't you afraid?" She looked at me in total amazement and said quietly, "Of course I'm afraid."

These girls are going out constantly among those "controlled" roads. Keep your fingers crossed.

Yet Peter Hunting from Dexter, Missouri, with International Volunteer Services in South Viet Nam, complains that there's too much talk about danger. It's keeping young men from volunteering for IVS in Viet Nam, he says; and IVS needs volunteers. There are only 40 IVS men in the whole country, and opportunity for ten times as many.

IVS is a small, private enterprise, the original Peace Corps some years older than the government-payroll one. Its young men work with USOM, but independently, on their own in remote places. They speak the local language fluently; that's the first thing they learn in IVS.

The Viet Cong's no bother, Peter Hunting says, unless maybe they'd hit your village in the night, but how safe are you on American highways? No IVS man has had any trouble with the Viet Cong; all you need is ordinary good sense. Any time they start moving someone tells you right away. They wreck schools and they may kill teachers, so you help get her out of the way and hide books and so on; then you just go in the other direction. And come back when they're gone.

The peasants are fine folks, you have the time of your life. You help them put up schoolhouses, dig wells, and so on. You live with them, just as they do; eat the food, drink the water—boiled of course. There are brick houses in every village, a couple of IVS men rent one and hire a woman to cook and keep house. The food is good; a little rice, plenty of fish and fruit and delicious vegetables of all kinds that haven't even a name in English. You feel fine. There's not much sanitation but the people are healthy because they eat right; Americans eat too much.

They're fighters, too. There was this village a few weeks go, only seven armed men in it. They saw about 250 Viet Cong coming in daylight, a mile or so away, down along a trail. So the seven went out and ambushed them. Fought a rear-guard action to give the men and women time to get in from the fields, into the hamlet. Hamlets have deep ditches dug around them, with sharpened bamboo stakes set in the ground, pointing out, on both sides of the ditch. So the seven got back in, with two wounded, and they held off the Viet Cong till troops got there. The villages have radios to call government troops. When they saw the helicopters the Viet Cong just vanished. The paratroopers are getting there faster than they used to, but it's hard to catch the Viet Cong.

What's important, Peter Hunting says, is the progress. It's wonderful. The people keep going right ahead. The standards of every village in his district are higher than they were two years ago. That's something to see. Peter Hunting's only complaint is the publicity about danger; it's exaggerated, and it's keeping men from volunteering for IVS in Viet Nam.

The USOM workers were going out from behind their guarded barricades, flying with Viet troops in military planes to provincial cities and refugee camps. USOM in Viet Nam is the largest unit of American civilian foreign aid in the world. In Saigon its hundreds of employees, one-third American, two-thirds Viet, occupy two huge buildings in separate compounds, a shuttle bus running between them.

Coming from the 19th century as I do, I cannot grasp the complexities of today's large organizations. But I did see that USOM workers *work.* I saw them patient in maddening difficulties, cheerful in discouragements, sincere in serving the Viet Government's department chiefs. Old-timers in USOM firmly check impetuous new-comers; they are not there to do *their* best for the Viets, they are there to help the Viets act for themselves, if asked.

In March there were hopes in USOM Agriculture of showing the most savage mountain tribesmen that water buffalo, now sacrifices to tribal gods, are also useful beasts of burden, and of introducing a well-drilling rig to hamlets now lacking water when summer springs go dry. In July the Viet Cong were destroying villages throughout the highlands; 537,000 refugees were counted, and more coming.

Public Health, USOM, retreated from villages but was still holding at district level, giving medical supplies and some personnel to Viet dispensaries and infirmaries outside the provincial capitals. In Saigon there were steadily more volunteers to training courses for nurses, sanitary agents, district health workers. When one course was filled, Miss Alice Frazer opened another. And another. A thousand nurses were graduated, more in training. USOM Education, too, was graduating teachers to be assigned in September when Gladys Philpott would be opening schools in village and refugee camps.

Saigon's southern suburbs melt into the Delta. Ages ago the mountains baffled the powerful Mekong River on its 3,300 mile way to the sea from the highest Himalayas in Tibet. So the river built a broad peninsula more than a hundred miles into the Gulf of Siam. Ho Chi Minh avidly covets these thousands of square miles of inexhaustibly fertile soil, always moist, always warm under the equatorial sun. The people forced into industry in North Viet Nam need the rice growing here.

The city-heart of the whole Delta is Can Tho, a growing-up village of some 80,000 people which sprawls along a bank of the wide Mekong. There are no tall buildings and Can Tho has an air of leisure, though building is going on and business is brisk in the miles-long market on the river bank where chattering crowds are buying and selling everything from Thai silks to flopping fish. Elegantly lettered street-corner signs ask and answer such questions as: "Who murders women and children? Viet Cong."

All public buildings are guarded. A soldier stands at the open gateway to USOM quarters, plain but sufficiently comfortable two-story buildings inside iron fencing. From here it is five minutes drive to the most renowned place now in the Delta: Can Tho Hospital.

Soldiers at its gate seem more symbolic than useful. Inside the compound are courtyards beyond cobbled courtyards and throngs of peasants. They are standing talking, they are moving in long lines into clinic and emergency ward, they are sitting in rows on the curbs of arcades. There are offices here and there, and a bewilderment of many shadowy wards in many buildings. In the smallest office Miss Beverly Ann Fry, R.N., presides calmly over all.

Miss Fry is from USOM Public Health. USOM is not in Viet Nam to care for the Viet people; USOM is there to help them, if they wish, to care for themselves. Miss Fry is not in Cam Tho to create an American hospital; the Viet people are intelligent and self-respecting, well able to make and manage hospitals in their own way. There are not enough doctors and nurses now, but there will be.

In Can Tho Hospital now the medical, surgical, children's wards hold many more patients than beds, and there are more wards than available nurses. An Australian surgical team of surgeons and anesthetists steadily working twelve hours a day employs nearly all the nurses in the hospital. I said, "But the government sending surgical teams should send nurses." Miss Fry said firmly, No. We are not there to impose a modern foreign hospital on the people; let them learn; they will learn, they want to. They will take what they want from others and they will do things well in their own way.

Famous Can Tho Hospital with its crowded, cluttered courtyards, its dark wards and haphazard ways certainly resembles nothing American. Three patients in one hospital bed—it's an appalling thought. But these are Viet beds, polished hardwood slabs, with a cool, thin, straw mat on each. The wards are dark because windowless walls shut out heat and the pitiless glare of the sun. In the pleasing dusk the beds hang on chains from the low ceiling and scores of almost naked patients lounge on them, chatting with each other and with relatives camped on the floor amid the beds. Four or five together leave a whole bed for one in a cast or taking a nap.

Slowly it dawns on you that here is a sociability and an acceptance of pain and illness as part of living which must be helpful in getting well. Can it be that Americans don't need as much technically trained authority and attention as we think we do? In Can Tho Hospital one nurse writes charts in two wards but mothers, sisters, wives sit by the beds. In the mornings Miss Fry walks by, seeing each patient she passes, now and then looking at a chart. Viet and American doctors are in the hospital, on call.

The vast hospital kitchen is thick-walled and moderately cool.

Down in its middle stretches the long brick table, pits for charcoal fires all along its length. Long ladles and forks, pans and pots of hand-hammered metal hang on a wall above wooden tables. The uneven floor is bricks. Steaming on the stove are caldrons of soups, sauces, vegetables, fish, rice, and water.

Against one long wall stand at least a dozen gleaming white porcelain dishwashers, a gift from private American helpfulness sent all the way to Cam Tho and of no earthly use in a place without electricity. Miss Fry, more genuinely grateful than I could be, still could not think what to do with the dishwashers. I said, "Sell them." She said, "To whom?"

The endlessly level plain around Can Tho is paved with oblong green fields and oblongs of water-covered growing rice. Networks of canals spread from the Mekong's six branches, each as broad, meandering and muddy as the Missouri below Yankton. More than half of Viet Nam's twelve and one-half million people live here in villages usually one homestead wide and miles long, hamlet touching hamlet along a canal shaded by wild jungle hedges and date and coconut palms, bananas, mango, custard apple and breadfruit trees. Protecting these thin, long villages from raiders is impossible.

But the Viets have done the impossible for longer than two thousand years. By any human measure of possibilities, their survival—as a distinct human type, as a culture, a way of being and believing—has been impossible since the third century B.C. They survive; they remain Viets. (Viet Nam means southern Viet: *nam* means south.)

In the second century B.C. the simple peasants in the Red River valley could not possibly resist the overwhelming force of the Chinese "human sea" and the far-superior Chinese culture which engulfed all that touched it. But they did. Chinese armies attacked them; and again; and again. After three centuries of fighting the Viets negotiated; they agreed to pay annual tribute to the Son of Heaven, thinking taxes cheaper than war. But they intended to continue governing themselves.

A bamboo hedge enclosed every village and no outside power came in. The Chinese named the country An-nam (the pacified south) and every century for a thousand years they suppressed a major Anamite revolt; meanwhile no official entered a village uninvited. Even a nine-button mandarin waited outside the bamboo hedge until the village chiefs came out to escort him ceremoniously in, offer him courtesy and tea and ceremoniously escort him out. Inside the bamboo hedge there was no Chinese census, no Chinese tax, no Chinese law. The village chiefs reported population and tax rates, formally; nobody imagined that they reported truthfully.

They adopted useful novelties from the Chinese: better methods of irrigation. Water buffalo, iron plow, bricks. Books, education. Bright young Viets studied the Chinese philosophers, passed the examinations, became mandarins. They were exempt from taxation, they were granted estates, they became rich; they did not become Chinese.

In the ninth century A.D. their tenth major rebellion succeeded; the Chinese retreated from the Red River valley and the Viets had Viet kings for four hundred years. Then the Mongols came.

No kingdom could stand against the Mongol hordes that conquered all kingdoms, across Asia from the China Sea to the Baltic, from the Arctic Circle to the Mediterranean and the Nile. Kublai Khan's warriors took China; 400,000 strong, they came down on the Red River valley and year after year 200,000 Viet peasants-in-arms drove them back. The Mongols did not conquer the Viets.

Fifteen years ago in wrecked seaports and ravished villages surely a peasant League for Independence could not possibly defeat the government of France returning with seasoned French, British, Indian and Japanese troops, the British navy, and American wealth. But the Viet Minh won at Dien Bien Phu.

These are historic facts. They baffle historians. The most keenly interested, most solidly informed scholar cannot explain the history of the Viet Nam people.

It can't be possible to protect from swift raiders a string of single houses 12 miles long, but the Viets were doing it when I was in the Delta. Two years earlier the Viet Cong had ruled the Delta firmly from Saigon to the Gulf of Siam. Now they lurked in its fringe of mangrove swamps. Three divisions of Viet troops were stationed at strategic points; they had Viet air support and radio communication with every village. The Viet Cong had learned that a raid, or even a movement, brought a quick air-strike and a flock of paratroopers dropping from helicopters. USOM workers were in the villages by day and at night the villagers' Self-Defense groups were out hunting Viet Cong in the dark.

There is something in these people that isn't explained, something that does not give up, that is not conquered.

The women, maybe? We know that even in places where women are downtrodden, nothing is ever done without us. And Viet women have never been downtrodden. Foremost among Viet Nam's heroes are the two sisters who led the first revolt against the Chinese 1,900 years ago. They freed the Viets and reigned as queens for a time; when the Chinese defeated them in battle they killed themselves. The next rebel leader was a woman, too. In Viet Nam now there are businesswomen, women attorneys, writers, doctors, soldiers, army officers.

They are said to be the most beautiful women in the world. In Paris, in Budapest, in Istanbul, even in San Francisco in the old days I have not seen as many such beautiful women as I saw in Saigon. They are not tall but perfectly proportioned, slenderly rounded, with slender hands and feet, bare feet on wooden sandals. Their smooth skin is not cream-yellow as Chinese skin is, not tanned-brown as Polynesian; it is golden, truly golden as the ring on your finger. You must see it to believe it. Their long hair is dense black, their eyes dark under straight upper lids, their lips remind you of a Greek statue's.

They move precisely, controlled, deft and quietly alert. They miss nothing and the slightest comedy delights them; their eyes laugh easily, before they smile. With a self-respect which I have been sad to see lacking in other countries, unanimously they wear their traditional dress. Nearly a century of French domination, French schooling, French language and literature and art, French theater and films, French fashion journals, and chic French women before their eyes did not lure them into Parisian clothes.

Elegant ladies, rich women, typists, secretaries, teachers, peasants, clerks, shopkeepers all wear the *ao dai.* This is a snugly fitted top, stiff-collared, long-sleeved, sewed to an ankle-length straight skirt slit on both sides from hem to waist. It is made of hand-woven silk, satin, chiffon, plain or brocaded, of every tint and color, dainty, brilliant, gorgeous. Under it are plain white or black trousers. You should see Saigon's streets at noon when the girls pour out of the offices, long hair loose, caught at the nape with a ribbon, and over all a total impression of good breeding, gracious decorum—the word is ladylike; I haven't heard of it since this century's teens.

The children in Viet Nam are remarkable, too. They crowd around an American in markets and refugee camps, as children do elsewhere, but they do not assail you, they don't whine or yell. They walk beside you quietly, by dozens, now and then glancing sidewise under lowered lashes. Meet a glance and the child ducks a shy little sidelong bow. Smile, and a roguish delight flashes back at you. These are slum children, peasant refugee children, in rags, almost naked. Their behavior says much for their mothers' characters; only children abundantly loved and strictly disciplined can be so well behaved, so self-confident, so endearing. As Gladys Philpott said: "I always want to put my arms around them all and take them home with me."

I saw little of Viet men; this is war and every office is on the battlefield. Those I met were courteous, quickly helpful, automatically friendly, preoccupied. I had only one glimpse of something more than worried working.

A whole clan of mountaineers, 1,200 men, women, children, had walked into Binh Dinh province, and the provincial security officers had settled them on vacant land. They were given rice, they seemed to be doing well. One night the Viet Cong took all of them, the whole clan, back into the mountains.

The security officers and USOM people discussed what could be done to prevent another such calamity. The talk was matter-of-fact; the feeling was tragic. The difficulty was too many refugees, too few men in the security force. Major Nguyen Be was exchanging courteous farewells when suddenly, as if a control broke, he said:

"Communism is *wrong!* So it is short term, it rises up swiftly as a quick flame, it is gone soon. As Hitler flared up and is gone. We stay; we survive. Because freedom is right and right is everlasting."

Selected Bibliography

Rose Wilder Lane's Nonfiction

"All Men Are Liars." *Woman's Day,* March 1940.

"America Enters Jerusalem." *Ladies Home Journal* 36 (April 1919): 7–8.

"Behind the Headlight." *San Francisco Bulletin,* October 9–November 5, 1915.

"Behind the Screens in Movie Land." *San Francisco Bulletin,* October 25–December 12, 1917.

"The Big Break at Folsom." *San Francisco Bulletin,* January 4–February 1, 1917.

"The Building of Hetch-Hetchy." *San Francisco Bulletin,* October 4–November 14, 1916.

"Christmas Editorial." *Woman's Day,* November 25, 1939.

"Christmas in Erivan." *Good Housekeeping,* December 1924.

"The City at Night." *San Francisco Bulletin,* April 30–May 16, 1917.

"Come into My Kitchen." *Woman's Day,* October 1960.

"Country Life." *Cosmopolitan,* June 1939.

"Credo." *Saturday Evening Post,* March 7, 1936.

Discovery of Freedom: Man's Struggle against Authority. 1943. Reprint, New York: Arno Press, 1972.

"Drive Like a Woman." *Good Housekeeping,* January 1939.

"Ed Monroe, Manhunter." *San Francisco Bulletin,* August 11–September 15, 1915.

"If I Could Live My Life Over Again." *Cosmopolitan* 78 (March 1925): 32.
"The Insidious Enemy." *Good Housekeeping* 71 (December 1920).
"Life and Jack London." *Sunset,* October 1917–1918.
"Out of Prison." *San Francisco Bulletin,* February 2–March 15, 1917.
"Out of the East Christ Came." *Good Housekeeping* 69 (November 1919).
"Own Your Own Home." *Woman's Day,* January 1939.
Peaks of Shala. New York: Harper, 1923.
"Rose Lane Says." *Pittsburgh Courier,* April 3, 1943.
"Rose Wilder Lane, by Herself." *Sunset* 41 (November 1918): 26.
"Should We Help Our Children Marry?" *Woman's Day,* March 1938.
"Soldiers of the Soil." *San Francisco Bulletin,* February 23–June 3, 1916.
The Story of Art Smith. San Francisco: *Bulletin,* 1915.
"Strange as Foreign Places." *McCalls* 49 (September 1919).
Travels with Zenobia: Paris to Albania by Model T Ford. (Cowritten with H. D. Boylston). Columbia: University of Missouri Press, 1983.
"War! What the Women of America Can Do to Prevent It!" *Woman's Day,* April 1939.
"A Woman's Place Is in the Home." *Ladies Home Journal,* October 1936.
"World Travelogue." *San Francisco Call & Bulletin,* April 10, 1938.

Scholarship and Other Writings

Anderson, William T. "Laura Ingalls Wilder and Rose Wilder Lane: The Continuing Collaboration." *South Dakota History* 16 (summer 1986): 89–143.
———. *Laura's Rose: The Story of Rose Wilder Lane.* De Smet, S.D.: Laura Ingalls Wilder Memorial Society, 1986.
———. "The Literary Apprenticeship of Laura Ingalls Wilder." *South Dakota History* 13 (winter 1983).
———. *The Little House Guidebook.* New York: HarperTrophy, 1996.
Anderson, William T., compiler. *Laura's Album: A Remembrance Scrapbook of Laura Ingalls Wilder.* New York: HarperCollins, 1998.
Bakken, Gordon Morris. *The Gendered West.* New York: Garland, 2001.
Botshon, Lisa, and Meredith Goldsmith, eds. *Middlebrow Moderns: Popular American Women Writers of the 1920s.* Boston: Northeastern University Press, 2003.

Ehrhardt, Julia C. *Writers of Conviction: The Personal Politics of Zona Gale, Dorothy Canfield Fisher, Rose Wilder Lane, and Josephine Herbst.* Columbia: University of Missouri Press, 2004.

Enstad, Nan. *Ladies of Labor, Girls of Adventure: Working Women, Popular Culture, and Labor Politics at the Turn of the Twentieth Century.* New York: Columbia University Press, 1999.

Fellman, Anita Clair. "Laura Ingalls Wilder and Rose Wilder Lane: The Politics of a Mother-Daughter Relationship." *Signs* 15, no. 3 (spring 1990): 535.

Helmbold, Lois Rita, and Ann Schofield. "Women's Labor History." *Reviews in American History* 17, no. 4 (December 1989): 501–18.

Hines, Stephen W. *I Remember Laura: America's Favorite Storyteller as Remembered by Her Family, Friends, and Neighbors.* Nashville: Thomas Nelson Publishers, 1994.

Holtz, William. *The Ghost in the Little House: A Life of Rose Wilder Lane.* Columbia: University of Missouri Press, 1993.

Lane, Rose Wilder, and Jasper Crane. *The Lady and the Tycoon: Letters of Rose Wilder Lane and Jasper Crane.* Caldwell, Idaho: Caxton Printers, 1973.

Lane, Rose Wilder, and Roger Lea MacBride. *Rose Wilder Lane.* New York: Stein and Day, 1980.

Lauters, Amy Mattson. "Rediscovering Rose Wilder Lane, Literary Journalist." Paper presented to the American Journalism Historians Association annual conference, October 5, 2004, Cleveland, Ohio.

———. "'Why Should I Stay?': Rural Woman's Voice through Laura Ingalls Wilder, 1911–1926." Paper presented to the American Journalism Historians Association annual conference, October 5, 2002, Nashville, Tennessee.

McElroy, Wendy. *Freedom, Feminism, and the State: An Overview of Individualist Feminism.* Washington, D.C.: Cato Institute, 1982.

Miller, John E. *Becoming Laura Ingalls Wilder: The Woman behind the Legend.* Columbia: University of Missouri Press, 1998.

———. *Laura Ingalls Wilder's Little Town: Where History and Literature Meet.* Columbia: University of Missouri Press, 1994.

———. "Rose Wilder Lane and Thomas Hart Benton: A Turn toward History during the 1930s." *American Studies* 37, no. 2 (fall 1996): 83–102.

Romines, Ann. *Constructing the Little House: Gender, Culture, and Laura Ingalls Wilder.* Amherst: University of Massachusetts Press, 1997.

Thompson, Dorothy, and Rose Wilder Lane. *Dorothy Thompson and Rose Wilder Lane: Forty Years of Friendship: Letters, 1921–1960,* ed. William Holtz. Columbia: University of Missouri Press, 1991.

Wilder, Laura Ingalls. *Laura Ingalls Wilder Country Cookbook.* Commentary by William Anderson. New York: HarperTrophy, 1995.

———. *The Little House in the Ozarks: Rediscovered Writings,* ed. Stephen W. Hines. Nashville: Thomas Nelson Publishers, 1991.

———. *West from Home: Letters of Laura Ingalls Wilder, San Francisco, 1915,* ed. Roger Lea MacBride. New York: HarperCollins, 1974.

Wilder, Laura Ingalls, and Rose Wilder Lane. *A Little House Reader,* ed. William Anderson. New York: HarperCollins, 2000.

———. *A Little House Sampler,* ed. William Anderson. New York: HarperCollins, 1988.